MODERN
NATIONS
—OF THE—
WORLD

AFGHANISTAN

MODERN
NATIONS
—OF THE—
WORLD

AFGHANISTAN

BY LAUREL CORONA

LUCENT BOOKS
SAN DIEGO, CALIFORNIA

THOMSON
———★———™
GALE

Detroit • New York • San Diego • San Francisco
Boston • New Haven, Conn. • Waterville, Maine
London • Munich

Library of Congress Cataloging-in-Publication Data

Corona, Laurel, 1949– .
  Afghanistan / by Laurel Corona.
    p. cm. — (Modern nations of the world)
  Includes bibliographical references and index.
  Summary: Discusses the people, land, culture, history, and future of the
  nation of Afghanistan.
    ISBN 1-59018-217-0 (hardback : alk. paper)
  1. Afghanistan—Juvenile literature. [1. Afghanistan.] I. Title. II. Series.
  DS351.5 .C67 2002
  958.1—dc21
                                                                2002003615

Copyright 2002 by Lucent Books,
an imprint of The Gale Group
10911 Technology Place San Diego, CA 92127
Printed in the U.S.A.

CONTENTS

INTRODUCTION

AFGHANISTAN AT THE CROSSROADS

"Geography shapes history; men only add a little color to its surface."[1] This observation by travel writer and explorer Jason Elliot was made specifically about Afghanistan, and nowhere on earth is its truth clearer. In this country of nearly impenetrable mountains and stark plains, an unusual blend of isolation from and contact with other groups has produced an astonishing and often bewildering variety of cultures that were only recently, and somewhat reluctantly, brought together as a nation. Landlocked within the region known as Central Asia, Afghanistan's forbidding geography makes it, for many travelers, a country to go around if possible, or, in the modern era, to fly over en route to somewhere else. Left alone by the outside world to tend to its own affairs, it would be one of the most isolated places on earth, and in many respects it still is.

THE CROSSROADS OF TRADE AND EMPIRE

Yet for centuries, various people have come to the land once known as Ariana and today called Afghanistan. Their presence has had a profound influence on its history and its current state of affairs. For centuries, Afghanistan was an important center for trade, strategically located along the overland route known as the Silk Road, from China to the Mediterranean. The area was also an important crossroads for foreign invaders, such as the Mongols in the thirteenth century, who usually stopped through on their way to bigger prizes. Thus, over time, the people of Afghanistan became a mix of many ethnic groups and adopted a number of different religious and cultural practices.

Because of the difficult terrain, travelers through Afghanistan had to want to undertake the journey very badly, usually for military or economic gain. Indigenous peoples, other than the nomadic groups, generally stayed close to home. As a result, the various communities of Afghanistan evolved in isolation from each other. Today, the nation is still a patchwork of ethnic groups separated by cultural, religious, and even physical differences that have become magnified in importance through the generations.

When travel over the Silk Road eventually dwindled in favor of sea routes, Afghanistan became an isolated country—until a nineteenth-century rivalry erupted between two aggressive empires bent on keeping the other from growing. The Russian Empire was pushing south from its Central Asian territories, and the British Empire was expanding north from India and what is now Pakistan. As a result of the consequent bloodshed and betrayals of what became known as the "Great Game," many in Afghanistan developed an intense suspicion of outsiders and a greater desire for isolation. Later, in the 1980s, a long, bloody, and ultimately unsuccessful attempt by the Soviet Union to subjugate Afghanistan made the country even more wary of foreigners. In 2001, American troops moved on to Afghan soil, and despite their common goal of overthrowing a repressive government that harbored international terrorists, the Afghan people as a whole remained ambivalent about the American presence in their country. In the Afghans' view, no

Isolated from society by the Dasht-i-Margo Desert, a lone hut stands on top of a barren hill.

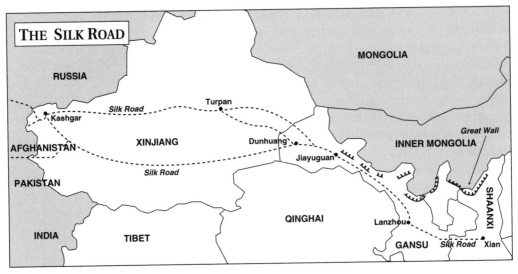

foreign power on their soil has ever come in friendship, and its presence has never failed to be destructive.

THE CROSSROADS OF RELIGION AND POLITICS

Another major contributing factor to Afghans' mistrust of outsiders is their intense devotion to their religion, Islam. Many Muslims, people who practice Islam, feel that the religion has been corrupted by too much contact with Western values and practices. They view the West, and particularly the United States, as having lost its spiritual direction in its pursuit of money. Others see the situation differently. Because of the lack of universities in Afghanistan, many Afghans go abroad for professional training and advanced education. A large number never return from their schooling in London, New York, Berlin, and elsewhere, deciding there is no reason to live without modern conveniences for what seems to them to be questionable spiritual superiority. As a result, many of the more moderate political voices have been lost within Afghanistan, making the more radical voices louder, clearer, and more powerful.

In 1996, after years of devastating civil war in the wake of the Soviet withdrawal, a well-organized and well-funded group of fundamentalist Muslims calling themselves the Taliban took control of most of Afghanistan. The Taliban's severe interpretation of the Qur'an (Koran), the holy text of Islam, led it to cut back on the civil liberties of all Afghans, particularly women.

The Taliban also offered a hiding place and center of operations for terrorist groups and their leaders, including al-Qaeda, whose leader, Osama bin Laden, became Afghanistan's most famous "government guest." When their country became the first target of the new war on terrorism, declared after the September 11, 2001, terrorist attacks on the United States, typical Afghans had to endure a new round of destruction and bloodshed following on the heels of so many others in the last decades.

AT THE CROSSROADS OF THE FUTURE

With the fall of the Taliban and the installation in December 2001 of an interim government, many are hopeful that the country will enter a period of peace and recovery. However, centuries of divisiveness, coupled with periods of domination and attempted conquest by foreign countries, have left Afghanistan without a strong background in peaceful self-rule. Even their religion, Islam, is a divisive force. Although it binds almost all Afghans together in one sense, and creates a strong sense of commonality with Muslims worldwide, deep-seated disagreements and centuries-old struggles between the Shiite and Sunni divisions of Islam are a contributing factor to many of the internal conflicts in the country.

Afghans want a country ruled by Islamic moral concepts and traditions, but there are drastic differences of opinion about what this means. Some feel that the Qur'an contains all the direction a society requires. They believe in shari'a, or Islamic law, according to which a group of mullahs, or holy men, make political and social decisions as they see fit. Others say that a modern nation must be governed by a written body of laws universally applied to all citizens, rather than by a group of men who make legal and political decisions based on their interpretation of the holy text of their faith. This dispute has had, and will continue to have, a major effect on such important issues as the rights of women and the kind of education children receive. Though few in the post-Taliban era are likely to propose that shari'a play as large a role as it has in recent years, the importance of the Qur'an will keep it a powerful force.

There is very little, it seems, that Afghans agree about. Though many recently came together around the perceived need to rid the country of the Taliban, to interpret this as a birth of national unity would be a mistake. There is also no common view about what Afghanistan should strive for in the future. The question now for the interim government of Hamid Karzai, and the elected government that will follow, is whether Afghanistan and the world community can find a way to get this nation on its feet again on its own terms—that is, if Afghans can agree on what those terms are.

THE SHAPE OF A NATION: LAND AND PEOPLE

Afghanistan is located where Central Asia begins its rise to eventually become the Himalayas, the world's tallest and largest mountain range. Its geography is a mix of jagged and forbidding peaks; high, dry plains known as steppes; and a huge desert. Almost all the land of Afghanistan, therefore, presents difficulties for those who live there. Only a little more than 10 percent of the land in the entire country is suitable for cultivation, and much of even this tiny percentage requires irrigation systems relying on nearby rivers or springs.

It is hardly surprising, then, that the people of Afghanistan are hardy and expect little in their lives to be easy or pleasant. Survival has dictated that extended families take care of their own, and this support often extends, particularly in rural parts of the country, to all members of one's own ethnic group or clan. The difficulty of survival, however, has also prompted

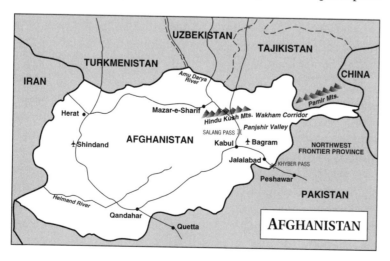

suspicion, prejudice, and sometimes hostility between ethnic groups who must compete for the resources that do exist.

THE HINDU KUSH

This lack of a common identity is quite natural considering Afghanistan's terrain. Two-thirds of the country is composed of mountain ranges at the western end of the Hindu Kush, one of the most rugged and forbidding mountain regions in the world. A look at the map of Afghanistan shows clearly that not only are mountains the major geographical feature of the country, but many cities, including the capital, Kabul, are isolated from each other by mountain ranges. Smaller mountain communities, some with only a few dozen inhabitants, are so remote that contact with the outside world is limited to the occasional privately owned truck passing through, loaded with anyone along the route who needs a ride. The roads in the mountains often are little more than one-lane trails hugging steep cliffs, and many of the valleys below are littered with the rusting remains of Soviet tanks and other vehicles that tumbled over the side.

Those who visit these mountains rarely fail to be moved by their grandeur. Vegetation is scarce, and the air is thin and clear, making the light and shadow at different times of day and year play off the colors of the jagged, bare rocks in infinite patterns that astonish with their beauty. Wherever vegetation manages to take hold, either naturally from water runoff or in areas cultivated by diverting water from springs, small settlements of people struggle to make a living as shepherds and growers of meager crops. Trips to larger communities to sell products such as apples and animal skins enable them to survive much as they have for centuries.

Many different ethnic groups and subgroups live in the mountains. Three of these groups are the Hazara, the Shiite Tajiks, and the Nuristani. The Hazara, also a Shiite group, are believed to have come to the area with Genghis Khan, the great Mongol warrior who came from China in the thirteenth century, and they retain a distinctly Asian appearance. Most are shepherds, although some grow meager crops using spring water. The Hazara live deep in the mountains west of Kabul, and many end up leaving their homes to seek menial work there or join the army, because life is so hard at home.

The Tajiks are one of the major ethnic groups in Afghanistan. The majority are urban dwellers, but a small subgroup lives in the mountains of the Badakhshan, the finger of land stretching eastward between Tajikistan to the north and Pakistan to the south. This group is isolated from other Tajiks by the fact that they are part of the Shiite branch of Islam. Shiite Muslims originally split from Sunni Muslims, the main branch of Islam in Afghanistan, over disagreements about how the successor of Mohammad, the founder and prophet of Islam, should be chosen. Over the centuries, opposing Sunni and Shiite views and cultures have widened the gap between the two groups. In Afghanistan, Shiite Muslims are the minority and are often persecuted and discriminated against. Because of their remote location and their faith, Tajik Shiites are one of the most alienated groups in Afghanistan today.

The Nuristani live in wooded areas in the rugged mountains east of Kabul. Their origin is unknown and somewhat mysterious: They look like people of the southern Mediterranean, but their language is a variant of the Sanskrit of northern India. The Nuristani are often referred to as *kafirs,* or unbelievers, because they did not become Muslim until a little over a hundred years ago, in 1896, when they were forced to convert by King Abdor Rahman. Very resistant to contact with outsiders, they remain one of the least-known cultures in the country.

THE DESERTS

The mountains are not the only environment in Afghanistan hostile to human habitation. The southwest corner of the country, with an average altitude of fifteen hundred to two thousand feet, is composed of forty thousand square miles of desert, known as the Dasht-i-Margo (Margow Desert) in its southern stretches and the Dasht-i-Khash (Khash Desert) to the north. Its climate extremes are so severe year-round that water typically freezes at night even when day temperatures reach as high as 120 degrees. Annual rainfall in the entire country averages only seven inches, but it rains even less in the desert areas. These extremes of temperature and limited rainfall make the deserts unsuited for agricultural development.

Several rivers cross the desert, including the Khash Rud, the Farah Rud, and the Helmand River, which, at seven hundred miles long, is the largest river entirely within Afghanistan. The

A camel carcass decomposes in the hostile Afghan desert where extreme temperatures make the land uninhabitable.

Helmand River ends in large, marshy Lake Helmand on the Iranian border. The lake grows and shrinks over the year depending on rainfall in the mountains that feed the Helmand River. Other marshy areas exist in southwest Afghanistan, but all these waters are too brackish to provide much in the way of food or irrigation.

Small towns dot the banks of the Helmand River, but no major population centers are found in the Afghan desert. The inhabitants there are mostly Pashtun, who make up somewhere between a third and a half of the total population in the country and live primarily in the southern regions. Their traditional territory spills over into neighboring Pakistan and Iran, homes to another seven million Pashtuns. The Pashtuns regard themselves as the true Afghans, having come out of the mountains in the eleventh century to help the Ghaznavid dynasty conquer India. The two major Pashtun groups, the Ghilzai and the Durrani (also called Abdali), are the most politically powerful in the country, having produced all but one of its leaders.

THE STEPPES

The Pashtuns have expanded their influence by living in increasing numbers in the north, an area of high plains called steppes, characterized by dry, grassy vegetation and a few shrubs. The Sunni Tajiks, however, known as artisans, farmers, and traders, and centered in the Herat and Kabul areas, are the main population group in the northern steppes. The Tajiks, who originated in Iran, are the second largest ethnic group in Afghanistan after the Pashtun; there are 4 million Tajiks in Afghanistan, another 1.5 million in Tajikistan, and another million in Uzbekistan.

Another major ethnic group in northern Afghanistan is the 1.5 million strong Uzbeks, who are primarily farmers and animal breeders, and trace their roots to the Central Asian Turks, or Tatars. Like several other groups in Afghanistan, the Uzbeks, who have given their name to the country of Uzbekistan, have traditionally occupied lands that today are part of more than one nation, and this has been one of the complicating factors in getting them to see themselves as Afghans. They identify

NOMADS

Approximately one in seven people living in Afghanistan today is nomadic or seminomadic. True nomads have no permanent home base, spending their lives moving from place to place and living in tents; seminomads, on the other hand, have a home base that they leave for substantial portions of the year. Both groups maintain their existence by leading their flocks to pastures all over the region and engaging in trade in the cities and towns on their route.

The best-known group of Afghan nomads is the Powindah, ethnic Pashtuns, also known as the Kachi. Until 1961, their annual migration took them well outside the borders of Afghanistan to Pakistan, where they sold wool and animal skins and brought back goods for their use or resale. A border dispute in 1961 put an end to their ability to go to Pakistan, but they continue to roam within the boundaries of Afghanistan. Powindah men are tall, with large mustaches, and sport big turbans, daggers, and rifles. As is customary among many nomadic peoples, the women wear a great deal of jewelry. Among the Powindah, the jewelry is mostly silver and adorns wrists, ankles, and noses. The women cover their heads with shawls and wear trousers and brightly colored tops.

Nomads continue to live much as they have for centuries and are among the Afghans most resistant to change. They have a strong dislike for city dwellers. In fact, one of the ways a mother scolds a daughter she feels is out of line is to tell her "may you marry a city dweller."

most strongly with the region where their ethnic group pre-
dominates, rather than with a nation whose other citizens often seem strange and foreign to them.

The steppe areas, particularly in the north and in the region
stretching south and east from Kabul, are the most productive
agricultural regions in the country. The northern plains, which
extend to the Turkmenistan, Tajikistan, and Uzbekistan borders, are the largest agricultural area. The Amu Dar'ya River,
which forms part of the northern Afghan border, is fifteen hundred miles long. The largest and longest river in the country, it
eventually empties into the Aral Sea in Turkmenistan. The waters of the Amu Dar'ya allow for the irrigation of crops, primarily rice and cotton, in the area around the historic cities of
Balkh, Mazar-e Sharif, and Konduz. Good pastureland permits
grazing of sheep and goats. At the opposite corner of the country, the Kabul River, 320 miles long, provides another important
source of water. Its waters irrigate a small but growing area
around the Khyber Pass, which borders Pakistan.

KABUL

All of Afghanistan's cities lie in the steppe regions or the
foothills of the Hindu Kush, where the climate is more hos-
pitable and travel is relatively easier. Kabul, the capital city, is
nestled between two ranges of the Hindu Kush. Its setting and
climate are sometimes compared to those of Denver, Col-
orado. Kabul has dry summers, rainy springs, and winters with
such heavy snowfall that the city can become snowbound.
Nevertheless, it has one of the best overall climates in the
whole country, compared to the extreme heat and cold of the
mountains and deserts. It is often said that climate in
Afghanistan is largely a matter of altitude, with the most pleasant regions being between the extreme lows and extreme
highs of elevation.

Kabul is a city of contrasts. Along its streets, private cars,
gaily painted buses, and armored vehicles jostle to pass between camels, donkeys, and horse-drawn carts all laden with
goods for the many bazaars in the city. An unusual character-
istic of these bazaars, whether open-air or covered, is that they
are strictly organized by the type of product. Vendors do not sell
an assortment of products in one place, so to purchase grains,
vegetables, carpets, leather goods, or pots and pans, shoppers
know to go to particular spots. In recent years, some of the

older bazaars have been torn down and replaced with more modern two- or three-story buildings consisting of a shop on the ground floor and living space above.

A horse-drawn cart passes shops in a bazaar in Kabul.

The city is divided into an old section and a newer section. The area south of the Kabul River, known as the Shari Kuhna, or Old City, contains the more historic sites. The area north of the river is home to most of the embassies and parks and the Royal Palace. The kind of diversity usually seen in cities with old and new sections is not apparent in Kabul today, or in the other cities in the country. The aftermath of decades of war is that very little, old or new, is left standing in its original form in Kabul. In fact, one recent map shows the location of various buildings, but adds in eye-catching red ink "ATTENTION: In the last years most of Kabul has been destroyed."[2]

QANDAHAR

At the end of the U.S. efforts to unseat the Taliban government in 2001, the focus of military action shifted to Qandahar, one of the most important cities in Afghanistan and the original home of the Taliban. Qandahar, which was the first capital of modern Afghanistan, lies in the southeast of the country, where the mountains finally, and rather suddenly, give way to desert. The area around Qandahar is well enough endowed with river water to grow crops, and for that reason, and because it is free of snow year-round, it is one of the biggest producers of fruit and timber, and one of the richest cities in the country. It is also one of the most picturesque, with cobbled streets, big bazaars, and an ancient walled city at its center. Because of its historic significance and its overall charm, Qandahar was a popular travel destination before war isolated Afghanistan and tourism ceased.

AFGHANISTAN'S OTHER CITIES

Two other cities are of particular importance in Afghanistan. Mazar-e Sharif is the largest city in northern Afghanistan and an important trading center. It is located just south of the Amu Dar'ya River, making it an agricultural center. Mazar-e Sharif is revered throughout the Islamic world as the place where Ali, the son-in-law of Muhammad and one of Islam's early leaders, is buried in a beautiful tomb.

Situated on the Herrud River in the Rud Valley, between the northwestern fingertips of the massive Hindu Kush mountain range, is the city of Herat, the center of a major fruit- and grain-growing area. Herat is also one of the major historic sites in Afghanistan, containing an old city surrounded by a moat and massive walls with many towers. Herat became a center of trade with Iran in the fifteenth and sixteenth centuries and is still a major producer of carpets and woolen goods. Herat was particularly hard hit during the Soviet occupation in the 1980s, when approximately two-thirds of its population fled or were killed. The city today retains little of its former energy or glory.

Several other cities constitute the rest of the major population centers in the country. Ghazni, an important commercial center lying eighty miles south of Kabul, is the former capital city of the rulers of the Ghaznavid dynasty in the tenth through twelfth centuries. Jalalabad is another historic city located on what is called the Grand Trunk Road between Kabul and the Khyber Pass, which serves as a border crossing point between

Afghanistan and Pakistan. Konduz is an important northern city located east of Mazar-e Sharif and just south of the Afghan border with Tajikistan.

Life in Afghanistan is made up of widely varying human experiences, created in large degree by its geography. However, in recent years, the isolating effect of geography has been reduced. War disrupts populations, causing people to flee their homes and settle in places where they are brought into contact with others. In addition, military service throws young men of varying ethnic groups together. Survival sometimes makes working together more important than harboring old

The tomb of Ali, in Mazar-e Sharif is revered throughout the Islamic world.

BALKH

At one time called "the mother of cities," the fabled trading town of Balkh, in northern Afghanistan, was an important stop on the Silk Road between China and the Mediterranean. It was already centuries old when it was destroyed by Genghis Khan in the thirteenth-century Mongol invasion. Today, Balkh is abandoned, according to Ralph H. Magnus and Eden Naby, authors of *Afghanistan: Mullah, Marx, and Mujahid,* and "surrounded by a crumbling but impressive outer wall in the middle of a vast, well-watered plain. Broken glazed tiles . . . and the foundations of bazaars, inns, and mosques attest to its lost fortunes."

Although some Afghan cities were able to recover their former prosperity in the centuries after the Mongol devastation, Balkh never did. This is in large part because twenty miles away, on a new and better road, the city of Mazar-e Sharif sprung up, diverting both traders and religious pilgrims away from Balkh.

With the resumption of tourism that is likely to occur if peace and security can be maintained in the post-Taliban era, Balkh is likely to see new prosperity as a tourist attraction for those who seek glimpses of a remote human past.

hostilities. The alliance that overthrew the Taliban was made up of many groups, and perhaps as the new century dawns, Afghans will find themselves identifying more as a nation. It is likely, however, that ethnic, regional, and cultural differences will continue to characterize a nation in which experiences will remain diverse.

CRADLE TO COLONY

Afghanistan is a land where time appears to lose at least some of its meaning. The sandy deserts and craggy mountains seem as if they have always been and always will be just the way they are now. The dress and traditional lifestyle of many of the ethnic groups in the country also provide a sense of timelessness. Afghanistan seems, in many respects, like an ancient culture that has found itself thrust into modern times.

The various ethnic groups in modern-day Afghanistan have all lived there for centuries. Many still cling to traditional ways because the land and their way of life have shaped who they are so completely that, despite the hardships, it is difficult to imagine living anywhere else. Traditional societies in isolated places tend to have long memories of past glories and defeats and, in some cases, of centuries-long feuds. Afghanistan's history is no exception: It is a tale of ongoing clashes between ethnic groups and loyalties within them, a story of shifting alliances and shifting borders.

Also, because of its location, Afghanistan has played host, sometimes willingly and sometimes not, to a number of foreign cultures over the centuries. Some of these outsiders have simply passed through on trade routes; others have swept through in their bids to conquer the world beyond Afghanistan; and still others have specifically made subjugating Afghanistan their target. Whatever the motive, these groups have also had a profound influence on Afghan history.

EARLY HISTORY

Today's Afghanistan is located very near what is commonly called the "cradle of human civilization," Mesopotamia. The whole region is of immense interest to archaeologists studying the evolution and spread of early human institutions such as cities and agriculture. People living in the area of present-day Afghanistan used tools made of sticks and stones in the sixth and fifth millennia B.C., but they had developed farming and livestock-breeding techniques by the fourth and third

21

millennia B.C. They also were casting iron in molds to make weapons and tools, and using a potter's wheel to turn out very technically advanced bowls and pots.

The similarity of these artifacts with those found in other parts of the Middle East, and the common roots of Afghan languages with those of Iran and India, suggest that there was already a great deal of contact with other cultures over a wide area at this point in history. The ruins of the third- to second-millennium B.C. city of Mundigak, near present-day Qandahar, suggest that Mundigak was an important provincial capital at the dawn of recorded history. Other evidence suggests that the city of Kabul has been in existence since somewhere around 2000 B.C.

Nevertheless, Afghanistan was still on the outskirts of the major civilizations of the Middle East. This changed when Vishtaspa, a powerful ruler in Bactria, as part of Afghanistan was previously known, fell under the influence of a Persian preacher and reformer named Zarathustra, or Zoroaster, somewhere between 1400 and 600 B.C. Zoroaster founded the faith of Zoroastrianism, which sees the world as ruled by both good and evil forces. Zoroastrians believe humans are free to choose between these, but they will be held accountable upon their death for their good and bad actions. Zoroaster also was one of the first to acknowledge the importance of having laws and practices that would ensure a smoothly functioning society. He felt that the welfare of people was best served by having a very strong ruler who could both enforce laws and protect the land.

The leaders of the Achaemenian dynasty, the first in the region of Afghanistan, were Zoroastrians. The dynasty's key figures were Cyrus II the Great, who was the first to establish authority over the whole region, and Darius the Great, who ruled from 522 to 486 B.C. and expanded power all the way to the Indus River, east of Afghanistan's border today. Alexander the Great, one of the major world leaders and conquerors, eventually overthrew the Achaemenian dynasty in 329 B.C., establishing a Greek presence in the region that can still be seen vividly today in the ruins at Ay Khanom, near the Amu Dar'ya River. Alexander the Great's conquest also included the area around Qandahar and Kabul, extending as far east as the Punjab in present-day Pakistan. The Greeks ruled uneasily for several centuries, never really man-

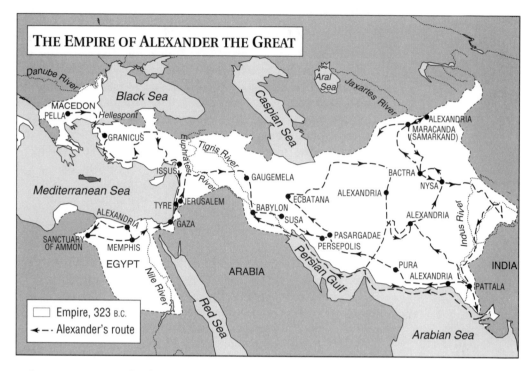

THE EMPIRE OF ALEXANDER THE GREAT

Danube River

Black Sea

Aral Sea

Jaxartes River

MACEDON
PELLA

Hellespont

GRANICUS

Caspian Sea

ALEXANDRIA
MARACANDA
(SAMARKAND)

Euphrates River

Tigris River

ISSUS

GAUGEMELA

BACTRA

NYSA

Mediterranean Sea

TYRE

JERUSALEM

BABYLON

ECBATANA

ALEXANDRIA

ALEXANDRIA

Indus River

ALEXANDRIA

GAZA

SUSA

PASARGADAE

PERSEPOLIS

SANCTUARY
OF AMMON

MEMPHIS

EGYPT

Nile River

ARABIA

Persian Gulf

PURA
ALEXANDRIA

INDIA

PATTALA

☐ Empire, 323 B.C.

◄–· Alexander's route

Red Sea

Arabian Sea

aging to conquer the hearts and minds of the local people. Bloody revolts were ongoing, and eventually the Greeks withdrew in 130 B.C.

The first few centuries A.D. were the era of the Kushan dynasty, which came into its full glory under one of its prominent rulers, Kaniska I, in the first century. At the time, the dynasty was widely acknowledged as being equal in power to Rome or China. The Kushan dynasty brought Buddhism, still only a few hundred years old, to Afghanistan, ushering in a new era of artistic excellence, religious tolerance, and cultural growth. Large quantities of foreign coins, particularly Roman ones, dating from the time of the Kushan dynasty are testimony to the region's importance as a trade center for the movement of goods between the Mediterranean and Asia.

THE FIRST ISLAMIC EMPIRES

The importance of Afghanistan as a crossroads for trade was not lost on the Arabs, who in the seventh century went out to build a world empire based on their new faith, Islam. They were able to sweep over large portions of North and East Africa as well as the Middle East in the first century after the

ZOROASTRIANISM

Zoroastrianism is the faith founded by Zoroaster, known as Zarathustra in his native Persian language. Zoroastrian tradition claims he lived in the sixth century B.C., but historians believe he is likely to have lived much earlier, between 1400 and 1000 B.C. When he was around the age of thirty, Zoroaster began to experience visions and trances in which he believed he saw and was taught by Ahura Mazda, his name for God. Zoroaster taught that there was only one God and that the world was a great struggle between two opposing spirits: good (Spenta Mainyu) and evil (Angra Mainyu). Ahura Mazda wished for humans to choose good and to fight evil in thoughts, words, and deeds, but humans were free to choose as they wished.

Zoroaster's teachings were not well received in his native Persia, present-day Iran. He made his first key convert, Vishtaspa, in Bactria, in what is now northern Afghanistan, and from there his teachings spread to India, where there is still a small community of about ninety thousand practicing Zoroastrians, known locally as Parsis. Another ten thousand are scattered across the Middle East.

Zoroastrian concepts are in some respects similar to those developed by the Hebrews around the same time, as recorded in the Old Testament of the Bible. For example, both claim that there is one God and that both good and evil forces contribute to the choices humans make. The reason why Judaism took hold to become a major world faith (and to serve as the foundation for both Christianity and Islam), and Zoroastrianism dwindled into a small sect lies in part in the history of the region. Shortly after Zoroaster's words were written down in the document known as the Avesta, Alexander the Great swept through the region and destroyed many libraries. Most of the Avesta was lost forever, and thus the chance to develop the faith was undermined. Centuries later, Zoroastrianism enjoyed another brief period of strength, only to give way to the overpowering influence of Islam.

---

death of Muhammad in 632 A.D. Despite the fact that in many other regions people had quickly converted to Islam, the Arabs found strong resistance in Afghanistan when they arrived in 652. Even when the new faith seemed to have been adopted, once the Arab army went on to another city or region, many "converts" quickly went back to their old ways.

Nevertheless, by the 800s, many individual communities and powerful local leaders had accepted Islam. In 962, the country was united under its first Islamic ruler, Alptegin. The empire he founded was centered in Ghazni, near Kabul, and was known as the Ghaznavid dynasty. Unlike the other dynasties since the Achaemenian, which had been ruled by outsiders who had expanded their territory to include Afghanistan, the Ghaznavid dynasty was homegrown, and its successes in expanding its territory were evidence that Afghanistan itself was an important power in the region, not just someone else's colony. Ghazni became an important and beautiful new capital city during this era.

The best-known Ghaznavid ruler was Mahmud, who came to power in 998 and ruled for over thirty years. At the time of his death in 1030, he had conquered the Punjab region in Pakistan and was in the process of seizing lands deep in India. The Ghaznavid dynasty lasted until 1140, when a local warlord attacked Ghazni and forced the last Ghaznavid ruler to yield power. The new dynasty, known as the Ghurids, continued the Ghaznavid conquest of much of India, which represents the high point of Afghan power in Central Asia. It was to be the last period of indigenous rule for many centuries.

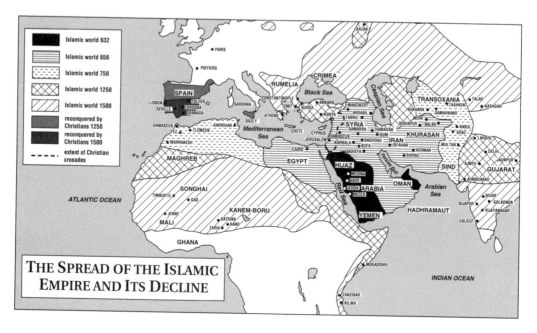

THE SPREAD OF THE ISLAMIC
EMPIRE AND ITS DECLINE

THE MONGOL INVASION

In 1219, the great Mongolian general Genghis Khan and his army continued their sweep from China to the Middle East by invading Afghanistan. Like others before him, Genghis Khan did not find conquering Afghanistan easy. In 1220, a group of Afghans under Jalal ad-Din Mingburnu defeated the Mongols in a battle near Kabul. Genghis Khan, who was away from his army at the time in Herat, was furious and vowed revenge against the Afghans. He laid siege to the city of Bamian, and when his grandson was killed in that siege, Genghis Khan gave orders to destroy Bamian and kill every last person there.

The Mongol conquest was a particularly destructive one. Cities, including Balkh, Herat, and Ghazni, were destroyed and their residents massacred. Deliberate attempts to destroy the culture and livelihoods of the people were also undertaken; in particular, painstakingly created irrigation systems were demolished. As a result, the small amounts of available agricultural land were largely ruined, turning the area into desert.

TIMUR AND HIS DESCENDANTS

Eventually, descendants of the Ghurid dynasty regained control, but not for long. In the wake of Genghis Khan, another great

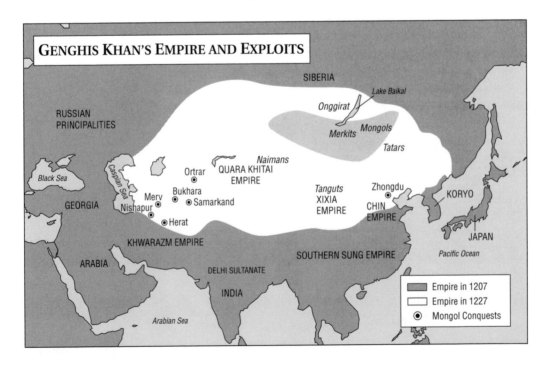

GENGHIS KHAN'S EMPIRE AND EXPLOITS

Asian empire builder burst on to the scene around 1370. Commonly known as Timur, or Tamerlane in English, from his full name Timour-I-Lang, he also found subjugating the Afghan people extraordinarily difficult, and he brought more death and destruction to the region. However, the Timurid dynasty, despite its violence, was not entirely negative. The Timurid era eventually became known as a golden age for arts and culture in the region, a time when poetry and miniature painting flourished, and beautiful new mosques and other buildings restored the glory of many cities.

The Timurid dynasty gave way in the early 1500s to the Mogul Empire under Babur, a descendant of Timur. Using Kabul as his base, Babur invaded India and established the Mogul Empire there. The Mogul Empire became one of the major cultural and political influences in Central and South Asia for several hundred years, but it set the Afghanistan region into decline. No longer were Kabul and other Afghan cities the centers of an empire. The Moguls concentrated on northern India, building monumental architecture and patronizing the arts there and largely ignoring their former base.

Mongolian general Genghis Khan led his army from China to the Middle East.

THE STRUGGLE FOR INDEPENDENCE

In the 1600s, the Persian Empire, based in present-day Iran, was expanding outward to the east, and in 1622 it took control of the area around Qandahar. The Afghan people found themselves the subjects of yet another foreign power. However, as throughout their history, they did not accept conquest without a fight. A century before, during the Mogul era, an Afghan leader named Bayazid Roshan began several decades of revolts, and his legacy was carried on throughout the 1600s by leaders such as Khushal Khan Khattak, an Afghan poet and warrior who led an unsuccessful nationwide uprising against the Persians.

MIR WAIS

Known affectionately as the "grandfather of his country" for his key role in moving Afghanistan toward nationhood in the eighteenth century, Mir Wais was the leader of the Hotaki tribe of Ghilzai Pashtuns located in Qandahar. At the time, the Qandahar region was part of the Persian Empire, and local tribal leaders were upset by the harshness of the appointed governor of the region, an outsider from the country of Georgia, far away on the Black Sea. Not only were there no cultural links with this leader, there was outright hostility: The current Persian dynasty, the Safavids, were Shiite Muslims and they were trying to impose this version of Islam on the Sunni Muslims of Qandahar. Differences between Sunni and Shiite Muslims are deep-seated, dating from shortly after the death of Muhammad in 632. Thus, this was a matter of dire importance to Mir Wais and his people.

For a brief period, Mir Wais was held as a hostage of the Safavid dynasty, but he engineered his escape by announcing he wished to go on a hajj, or pilgrimage to Mecca, one of the sacred duties of all Muslims. While in Mecca, he consulted with Sunni leaders, who gave him a fatwa, a legal opinion based on Islamic law, sanctioning a rebellion to overthrow the Safavid dynasty altogether. Mir Wais died of natural causes in 1715 at the age of forty-two, before this rebellion could be completed, but in the end, his descendants toppled the Safavid dynasty, thus ending the long period of Persian rule in Afghanistan that had begun in 1622. Mir Wais is buried in a beautiful mausoleum on the outskirts of Qandahar.

The portion of Afghanistan around Qandahar achieved independence from the Persian Empire in 1708 under Afghan ruler Mir Wais. In 1722, Mir Wais's son Mir Mahmud invaded Persia and occupied part of its territory, turning the tables on the Afghans' former rulers. But control shifted back to Persian leader Nader Shah, who took Herat after a siege in 1732 and occupied most of the Mogul Empire, from Ghazni and Kabul all the way to Delhi in India, by 1739. However, when Nader Shah was assassinated in 1747, Ahmad Abdali, an Afghan, took the opportunity to declare the independent nation of Afghanistan. Ahmad was elected king, or shah, by a Pashtun tribal assembly known as a Loya Jirgah in the same year, and thus was born the

Kingdom of Afghanistan. The dynasty founded by Ahmad Shah was known as the Durrani, a name many Pashtun Afghans still use to identify themselves.

A CONTESTED NATION

The establishment of the new kingdom did not put an end to the struggle to control the region. While Ahmad Shah greatly expanded the Afghan Empire both east and west, making it the greatest Muslim empire of its time, those at home did not wish to be ruled by anyone. They honored the centuries-old Pashtun tradition of electing a leader to be "first among equals," meaning that a ruler should not try to reign over other local leaders but simply be a unifying figure. This created confusion as to who was really in charge of what. The major regions of Afghanistan all had their own local warlords and jockeyed for power and land among themselves. Balances of power in the region shifted regularly, largely as a result of the personal capabilities of individual leaders.

Ahmad Shah's son, Timur Shah, and his son Zaman Shah did not have Ahmad's leadership skills, and they faced constant revolts when they took the throne. Mahmud, a brother of Zaman Shah, with the help of the ruler of Persia, was able to force his brother from power in 1801. But he ruled only two years before being forced from the throne by yet another brother, Shoja, who only ruled until 1809 before Mahmud was able to retake the throne. Meanwhile, local leaders ignored the monarchy for the most part and continued their own power struggles and petty wars among themselves. Local rulers took advantage of the confusion and tried to encroach on Afghanistan's borders from east and west.

Afghanistan was in a state of anarchy by 1800. However, in Europe, the opposite was true. A political and military giant, Napoléon Bonaparte, the emperor of France, had conquered much of the continent and the Mediterranean region, and his desire for global domination was clear. When the British learned that Napoléon was planning an invasion of India, with Czar Alexander of Russia, the British contacted Shah Shoja to discuss how to defend against this possibility. Eventually, a treaty of friendship was signed, signaling a rather vague alliance between the two countries. This first show of interest in Afghanistan by a European power would have far-reaching and violent consequences in the new century.

THE BARAKZAI DYNASTY

Shah Shoja, however, soon lost the throne, and his brother Mahmud Shah also fell from power in 1826 at the hands of Dost Mohammad Khan, the first leader of the Barakzai dynasty. This dynasty, the last in Afghanistan, would last a century and a half, until 1973, when Zahir Shah, who is still alive today, was deposed. Dost Mohammad ruled, with one interruption, for over thirty years until his death in 1863. His reign is characterized by some of the most significant events in Afghan history.

In the mid–nineteenth century, two of the world's great powers, Russia and Great Britain, were engaged in a conflict that came to be known as the "Great Game." The British had political and trade interests in India, and they felt threatened by Russian incursions southward into Central Asia. The British saw control of Afghanistan as critical to maintaining the balance of power in the region. However, they did not feel that Dost Mohammad was either powerful enough or friendly enough toward the British to resist Russia if it should decide to expand into Afghan territory. Thus, they embarked on a course of action that would soon lead to the first Anglo-Afghan War in 1839.

This war would signal a major shift in the politics and subsequent history of the region. Since the era of the invasions of Genghis Khan and Timur, Afghanistan and its neighbors had fought only among themselves over their own region. Now, for the first time in centuries, an outsider with no links to the region and with an agenda of its own that had nothing to do with the well-being of the country had set its sights on controlling Afghanistan.

IN THE CROSSFIRE OF WORLD HISTORY

By the beginning of the nineteenth century, Afghanistan had gone through centuries of shifting borders, a low level of national organization, and even occasional anarchy, punctuated with a few eras of strong leadership by a charismatic king, sometimes Afghan in origin and sometimes not. Not since the time of Timur had someone from far outside the region attempted to gain control of Afghanistan. Events in the early nineteenth century, however, set in motion a new legacy of outside interference that continues to the present day.

AFGHANISTAN ON THE WORLD STAGE

When Dost Mohammad, founder of the Barakzai dynasty, became the leader of Afghanistan in 1826, he focused on strengthening Afghanistan's defense of its territory against Persia and others. However, despite his desire to present a united front to the powers on Afghanistan's borders, the country lacked strong national unity because the regional warlords saw little to gain by giving up any of their autonomy.

From their capital cities thousands of miles away, the leaders of Russia and Great Britain observed Afghanistan with increasing interest. It was the era of colonialism, when European countries established colonies on other continents because it appeared that the only way to remain a top economic and political power in Europe was to dominate around the globe. Great Britain, for example, had taken control of the Indian subcontinent (which then included present-day Pakistan) and had a very profitable colony in operation there. Russia, already by far the largest country in the world, stretched from the edge of Scandinavia in the west to China in the east, and was eyeing Central Asian territories to the south. Acquiring lands in Central Asia would provide outlets to the Indian Ocean as well as new natural resources for the Russian economy.

Dost Mohammad Khan kneels in his chambers overlooking his Barakzai dynasty.

At the time, Russia and Great Britain were two of the most powerful empires in the world, and they saw control of Afghanistan as critical to achieving their economic and political aims. They each believed that Dost Mohammad Khan was a weak ruler who would probably be unable to force provincial leaders to go along with any treaties he made with foreign countries. It seemed wise to both Great Britain and Russia to take control of Afghanistan themselves. Great Britain did not really want to colonize the territory as it had with resource-rich India, but it knew that if Russia gained control, it would not be long before Russia used its position there to make a move on India. Great Britain, therefore, wanted Afghanistan to serve as a buffer, and it was not confident that Dost Mohammad had the power or the desire to help achieve this.

The Anglo-Afghan Wars

The British made a fateful decision shortly after Dost Mohammad took the throne, a choice that would result in great bloodshed and a legacy of mistrust of Europe and the West that continues in Afghanistan today. After diplomatic discussions with Dost Mohammad failed to produce a treaty or even an agreement of neutrality, the British decided to overthrow him and reinstall former Shah Shoja on the throne. The idea was that Shoja would owe allegiance to the British for their support, thus allowing the goal of British control over the area to be achieved. In 1839, British troops invaded Afghanistan in a successful attempt to put Shoja on the throne, signaling the beginning of what would become the first of three Anglo-Afghan wars. Dost Mohammad's family was captured by the British in 1840, forcing him to surrender and go into exile.

The national unity Dost Mohammad could not achieve as ruler briefly came to pass as the Afghans struggled against the British. In 1842, the British lost their control over the government when Shoja was killed in an uprising. The British forces tried to retreat back through the Khyber Pass into their Indian

Afghan rebels chase the British forces through Khyber Pass in the first Anglo-Afghan War.

colony after their leader was killed. This was accomplished by a seventeen-year-old Afghan, Akbar Khan, whose act of defiance has made him one of the country's national heroes. In one of the most remarkable campaigns in Afghan and British military history, 16,500 British soldiers and their 12,000 dependents were wiped out, not in large pitched battles but little by little through ambushes, killing of stragglers, sniper fire from clifftops, and other means. Only one ragged survivor on a staggering pony made it back to the British fort at Jalalabad, a tale dramatically told and retold in British history books. Later, the British did manage to reinvade, primarily for revenge, but they were pushed out again by the Afghans by the beginning of 1843. This signaled the end of the first Anglo-Afghan War.

Dost Mohammad Khan retook the throne and ruled until his death in 1863. Another period of instability followed as his sons jockeyed for the throne but could not unify the country or protect its borders. Great Britain and Russia continued to view the area with great interest, although neither attempted to grab territory. In 1873, Afghanistan negotiated a treaty with Russia that established a clear border between the two countries and included, in exchange for some Afghan land along the Amu Dar'ya River, a Russian agreement not to invade Afghan territory. When Afghanistan's relationship with Russia improved, the British began to worry. They did not trust that the new ruler, Dost Mohammad's son Sher Ali, would be able to remain neutral and thus keep Afghanistan a buffer state.

In another attempt to keep the Russians at bay, the British started the second Anglo-Afghan War in 1878. Sher Ali was unable to pull together a united defense and, while fleeing the country, died in Mazar-e Sharif in 1879. His son briefly inherited the throne before being deposed in 1880 by Abdor Rahman after the battle at Maiwand. Maiwand produced one of the great legends of Afghan history, Malalai. As the story is told, the Afghan warriors were retreating in defeat but Malalai used her veil and her stirring words to rally them back into battle, where they ultimately annihilated the British. After Maiwand, with Abdor Rahman on the throne, the British negotiated a withdrawal from Afghanistan on the condition that they be allowed to dictate Afghanistan's foreign affairs and that the Khyber Pass and substantial other lands would become part of Britain's Indian colony.

Over the next few decades, border agreements were negotiated and renegotiated with Russia, Great Britain, and Persia (present-day). As a result, Afghanistan lost much of its outlying territory but gained clear borders and agreements not to violate them. By the time Rahman Khan's son and successor, Habibollah, died in 1919, the country had taken on its geographical shape as a modern nation. However, the next ruler, Amanollah, resented the fact that the British dictated Afghanistan's foreign policy. He knew that Britain's involvement meant that Afghanistan was not really an independent nation. Amanollah invaded India as a way of announcing an end to British power over Afghanistan, prompting the third and final Anglo-Afghan War in 1919. Amanollah was successful in his objective. The Treaty of Rawalpindi in 1921 ended British control over Afghan affairs and established the country as fully independent.

Dost Mohammad Khan sits cross-legged reading over a land treaty with Russia that caused the second Anglo-Afghan War.

AMANOLLAH AND NADER KHAN

Before Amanollah's time, Habibollah had been the first to recognize that Afghanistan would be at an increasing disadvantage with foreign powers if it did not modernize. He founded schools, encouraged the development of factories, improved roads, and established a weekly newspaper. He introduced Western medicine, electricity, and automobiles to the country, and he invited intellectuals such as Mahmud beg Tarzi, who had been exiled during more conservative times, to return to Afghanistan to help promote modernization.

Habibollah's son Amanollah, who ruled until 1929, also supported fashioning an independent Afghanistan along more modern, Western lines. Amanollah, under Tarzi's influence, promoted the idea of a constitutional monarchy, in which there is a king but elected officials run the government. Amanollah was popular and respected throughout his reign for his willingness to put the development of a strong, well-functioning nation above his own personal power. However, resistance to reform was great among some groups, and Amanollah was deposed in 1929. Despite this, he retained a great deal of support. In the end, one of these supporters assassinated the new ruler, Nader Khan, in 1933, partly over the issue of reforms but also because his rule was repressive and retaliatory by comparison. Nader Khan's personality made him suspicious of others and isolated him from those whose support he needed.

ZAHIR SHAH

Nader's son Zahir came to the throne at the age of nineteen. Because he was so young, he stayed in the background while his uncle, Mahmoud Khan, made decisions for him, an arrangement Zahir found himself unable to end even when he reached a more advanced age. In 1964, a constitutional monarchy, severely limiting the ruler's powers, brought Afghanistan in line with other modern nations such as Great Britain and the Netherlands. The constitution banned royal family members from holding office, and Zahir was able to push Mahmoud Khan aside and come into his own right as a leader. Zahir Shah ruled for forty years, until 1973. He tried to modernize Afghanistan through projects to develop irrigation systems and highways. He also instituted social reforms that permitted women to enter the workforce, hold government positions, and study at universities. In addition, he began modernizing and strengthening the army, largely with aid from the Soviet Union.

Late in Zahir's rule, Afghanistan endured several years of drought, adding to the difficulties of survival for the typical Afghan. In addition, a movement to establish a separate independent Pashtun state, Pashtunistan, in the border region with Pakistan, undermined Zahir Shah's rule. While on a European vacation in 1973, Zahir was informed he had been deposed, ending not just the Barakzai dynasty but the monarchy itself. Afghanistan declared itself a republic, and the leader of the coup, Zahir's brother-in-law Mohammad Daud, took over the new role of president.

THE DURAND LINE AND PASHTUNISTAN

In 1893, the British, who controlled the area of present-day Pakistan as part of their colony in India, drew a clear national border between Afghanistan and their colony. This border became known as the Durand line, named after the Durand Treaty that established it. This border, like so many others elsewhere in the world during the colonial era, was drawn without concern for the people who lived in the region; it simply reflected what lands the colonial power controlled at that particular moment. The result was that ethnic groups often became divided between two countries in ways that made little sense to them. This was the case for the Pashtuns with the Durand line. Their traditional territory extended on both sides of this new border, and they were used to moving freely throughout the area. Suddenly they found themselves part of two separate governments, each Pashtun a citizen in one part and a foreigner in the other part of what they saw as their ancestral land.

This became a major problem for the Pashtun when Pakistan became a separate nation in 1947. In 1949, Afghanistan announced that it would no longer recognize the Durand line. The Pashtun, who referred to Pashtun territory in Pakistan as "occupied Afghanistan," proclaimed a separate nation of Pashtunistan, encompassing Pakistan's Northwest Frontier Province and other western borderlands. For a while, civil war seemed imminent. However, the nation of Pashtunistan was never recognized as a sovereign country by other nations in the world, and Pakistan retained the land east of the Durand line. Tensions have continued over the issue into the present day, with many still supporting the idea of an independent Pashtunistan, citing the many new central Asian republics such as Uzbekistan and Tajikistan as examples of lands based on the ethnic majority found there.

THE MARXIST EXPERIMENT

Eight years before the fall of the monarchy, a small group of Afghans had begun meeting secretly to discuss the best methods to develop their country along the lines of the Soviet Union, their neighbor to the north. Afghan Communists favored modernization but disapproved of the Western philosophy of capitalism, which stresses competition among individuals for personal financial profit. Instead, they wanted to see Afghanistan evolve based on the principles advocated by German philosopher Karl Marx, who argued that the ideal society is one where everyone works together for the benefit of the whole and no one becomes rich at someone else's expense. This philosophy, called Marxism, became the foundation for communism, already in place since the 1920s in the Soviet Union. Under communism, people work in factories, farms, mines, and other workplaces known as collectives. The government provides the needed machinery and supplies, and the workers give what they produce to the government. Because people do not work for themselves, the government is also responsible for making sure everyone has food, shelter, and other necessities.

The Soviet Union was pleased to see this attempt by Afghan Marxists to create a new Communist state. According to writer Pankaj Mishra in "The Making of Afghanistan," "Communism offered [Afghanistan] both a way of catching up with and resisting the West, and the ideology had a powerful, and often generous, sponsor in the Soviet Union."[3] Members of this Marxist group, known as the People's Democratic Party of Afghanistan (PDPA), ran successfully for election to parliament and began working to promote Marxist ideas. Mohammad Daud, though not a Communist himself, became aligned with this group because he thought they might help his own political future, and when Zahir Shah was overthrown in 1973, the Communists did indeed turn to Daud to be the new president and head of the government.

Afghan Communists, who tended to be members of the educated elite, had, from the very beginning, divided into two feuding factions in the PDPA: the Parcham (translated as "flag" or "banner") and the Khalq (translated as "people" or "masses"). Though there were ideological differences, the enmity between the two groups was largely the result of quarrels between their leaders over power; this infighting distracted both Parcham and Khalq from the goal of putting a Marxist system in place.

After the Communists helped Daud become president, he quickly tried to distance himself from those who had backed him, and to loosen the country's links with the Soviet Union. Daud was convinced that communism would not take hold in Afghanistan because it was a doomed effort "to weld the incoherent ethnic-tribal worlds of Afghanistan"[4] into a single, centrally managed society. The Khalq and Parcham factions briefly settled their differences and joined together to get rid of Daud, who was murdered in a 1978 coup.

THE AFGHAN CIVIL WAR

Once Daud had been replaced and more committed Marxists and pro-Soviets were in control of the government, they acted quickly to make up for lost time. They began with hastily conceived land reforms in which anyone with more than six acres of farmland had to give up the rest for redistribution to others. This angered many Afghans, not just because they saw the Marxists as destroyers of traditional ways, but also because agriculture was already so difficult in the country and the land reform idea seemed likely to create more problems.

Adding to the problem was the fact that Communists are associated with atheism and believe that social progress cannot be made as long as people look to prayer and devotion to God as a means of managing their lives and solving their problems. During the several decades that the monarchy, and then the republic, had been stressing modernization, concern had already been growing among many Afghans that life was changing too much and too quickly. They felt that devotion to Allah and focus on the Qur'an for guidance was taking a backseat to modern ideas. The Marxist government did not actually move to close mosques or suppress the practice of Islam; in fact, it wanted to find a way to create a society that included both Islam and Marxism. Nevertheless, the association of communism with atheism served to intensify many Afghans' fears that Islam would be undermined if the Marxists remained in power.

The country's leaders responded to this unrest with force, arresting and executing tens of thousands of ordinary citizens. Specially targeted were political and religious figures, teachers and student protesters, and certain ethnic minorities, such as the Hazara, who had long been persecuted by the Pashtun ruling class for their Shiite beliefs. As a result, by 1975, armed insurrections against the Marxist government began. At the heart

*Fearing an uprising,
Marxist leaders execute
Afghan citizens with
radical political or
religious beliefs.*

of these uprisings were Muslims whose motivation was to reestablish a society with Islamic beliefs and practices at its core. These fighters were known as the mujahideen, which means "those who strive." As resistance to the Marxist government grew over the next few years, seven different mujahideen groups emerged, united by the desire to return to traditional ways, but divided along ethnic and regional lines by a long history of mistrust of and dislike for each other.

THE WAR WITH THE SOVIET UNION

Uprisings among the masses were matched by quarrels within the PDPA itself. These quarrels often turned deadly. President

Nur Mohammad Taraki, who was closely aligned with the Soviet Union, was murdered in 1979 by supporters of Hafizullah Amin, who favored more moderate and slower-paced reforms. The murder of Taraki was deeply alarming to the Soviet Union, for it was becoming clear that the Marxist revolution it had hoped for was not going to occur. Furthermore, the mujahideen had grown in strength, and it seemed only a matter of time until a new, Islam-centered, unfriendly government would be in place in Afghanistan. The Soviets knew they needed to move quickly if they were to salvage the situation.

In December 1979, thousands of Soviet troops were airlifted into Kabul. The Soviets took over the government after first killing Hafizullah Amin. They put another hard-line Communist, Babrak Karmal, in his place as what is referred to as a "puppet" president, one who does the bidding of a foreign power rather than that of his own people. But the Soviets soon learned the same lesson the British had during the previous century. All over the country, guerrilla fighters resisted the Soviet army by whatever means they had at hand, and the country settled in for another prolonged period of bloodshed.

The invasion of Afghanistan came during the period known as the cold war, when the United States and other allies were engaged in a power struggle with the Soviet Union. After the Soviet invasion of Afghanistan, the United States and its other Western allies saw a chance to weaken the Soviet Union by involving it in a long, unwinnable war. In the early 1980s, the United States began supplying arms such as shoulder-fired missile launchers called "stingers" to the mujahideen. In fact, the United States, carried out one of the most massive covert operations in history, channeling $700 million a year into the Central Intelligence Agency for support of the mujahideen. Because these expenditures were hidden, the United States could claim not to be directly at war with the Soviet Union, but in fact it was a major sponsor of the conflict.

The mujahideen, based deep in the mountains, could not easily be captured or killed and could count on having enough arms and ammunition to keep fighting. Despite the stalemate, the Soviets refused to back down. Over time, many Afghans began joining the mujahideen, but not for reasons rooted in Islam or in anticommunism, or even to fight for their country's freedom. In a war-torn country, fighting simply became something for young men to do. Without a clear cause or goal, many mujahideen used their American-supplied weapons as a way to get whatever they wanted, and over time they became a source of terror for many Afghans.

At home in the Soviet Union, opposition to the war mounted because it had no clear goal and was costing thousands of lives. Clearly, the Afghans had the upper hand. They could go on resisting indefinitely because they were well financed, they were on familiar territory, and, for many, armed warfare was already a traditional way of life. But the Soviet Union was not willing to admit defeat at the hands of a country it considered backward and globally insignificant, so the occupation dragged on. Uprisings in Afghanistan were dealt with by arrests, torture, and execution of suspects. The countryside was bombed in an attempt to frighten people into submission, setting in motion a flood of refugees fleeing in many cases from both mujahideen and Soviet terrorism. Approximately 5 million of Afghanistan's total population of 16 million left the country during the ten-year Soviet occupation.

Afghan mujahideen sit atop a Russian tank they captured after chasing the Soviets out of Gardez.

Coming into the country in the mid-1980s were countless Muslims from other countries, responding to the opportunity to fight for a cause. For some, the cause was a holy war, or jihad. Delivering Afghanistan from its occupiers was considered a sacred duty that would bring pleasure to Allah and earthly honor to those involved. Others looked at the Soviet-Afghan war with a more jaded eye. They could use their guns to get whatever they wanted, and there were monetary rewards for killing Soviet soldiers. Others had a larger picture in mind. Among those who arrived during this period was terrorist leader Osama bin Laden, a Saudi Arabian who built boot camps for soldiers from as many as sixty other countries as a first step in his evolving plan for a worldwide jihad against the West. According to journalist Sarah Boxer, the foreigners who came to fight during the Soviet occupation "changed the look of the resistance and ultimately the look of Afghanistan."[5] With virtually unlimited human and military resources, the resistance to the Soviets became entrenched, but it also stopped being solely about a fight for the freedom and future of Afghanistan.

Though the mujahideen presented themselves to the world as freedom fighters, the situation had become far more complex. In many respects, it simply resembled business as usual, but with bigger and more deadly arms, in a country characterized throughout history by violent rivalries. However, unknown to people at the time, a period of even greater violence was just around the corner. Meeting privately, in small "study groups," just as the Marxists had done several decades before, was a group called the Taliban. Their vision for the country would bring still more hardship and tragedy in the years to come.

4

THE RISE AND FALL OF THE TALIBAN

In 1989, the Soviet Union, on the verge of collapse, gave up and withdrew from Afghanistan. Though many believed the Marxist government would immediately fall without the support of the Soviets, it hung on to power until 1992, in large part because no better alternatives were apparent, and because the central government had become largely irrelevant in the anarchy that ensued. The only thing the seven main mujahideen resistance groups had in common was their resentment of the foreign-influenced, totally ineffective, and out-of-touch Marxist government, but no one group seemed suited to lead a nation once their shared mission of toppling that government was accomplished.

According to author Pankaj Mishra, after the Soviet withdrawal "there wasn't much to celebrate in Afghanistan. The destruction of roads and agricultural land and the flight of more than five million people (the largest refugee population in the world) created a political and economic void. . . . Long subsidized by the United States and Saudi Arabia, [the mujahideen] now had to be self-financing."[6] They did this by a number of illicit activities such as drug trafficking and smuggling consumer goods, which led to increased violence among the factions warring to control these markets. Once the Soviets withdrew, the United States had achieved its objective and did not follow up with the economic, technological, educational, and other aid programs that might have put the devastated country on a more solid footing.

By this point, Afghanistan had endured two decades of civil war, but peace was still not at hand. Some mujahideen groups set up an interim government consisting of a council of fifty individuals and a president, Burhanuddin Rabbani. Almost immediately, the mujahideen began fighting among themselves, a situation that quickly escalated into violence far worse than that seen during the war against the Soviets. The Soviet targets

had generally been mujahideen strongholds and the mujahideen themselves, and therefore the countryside had suffered
the most. After the Soviet withdrawal, the various mujahideen
factions recognized that control of the country meant control of
the cities, where, despite years of war with the Soviets, schools,
mosques, and businesses had generally managed to stay open.
Now, however, violence came to the cities as well, causing great
loss of life and destruction of property. According to one source,
rocket attacks in 1994 by supporters of Gulbuddin Hekmatyar,
Rabbani's main rival, "killed more civilians in the capital city
than had died in ten years of anti-Communist jihad."[7]

THE RISE OF THE TALIBAN

While destruction and corruption reigned throughout the
country, Rabbani and Hekmatyar were locked in a power struggle that fractured the uneasy coalition government. Officially,
Afghanistan was one country under one government, but in
truth it functioned as a number of more or less independent regions technically answering to a central government that exer-
cised no real control. Though many small groups of mujahideen

*Refugee children kneel,
listening to the
teachings of Allah in a
Pakistani relief camp.*

MULLAH OMAR

Mullah Omar, the founder of the Taliban, is one of the most mysterious figures in recent Afghan history—so mysterious that there are a few who say he does not really exist. Only one grainy and blurred photograph of Mullah Omar exists because he refuses to allow his picture to be taken and he is almost never seen in public. Stories about him abound, but their accuracy is often challenged. The Taliban has circulated stories designed to identify him with other legendary freedom fighters in Afghan history such as Malalai and Akbar Khan and to enhance his status as a moral leader. Some of these stories do appear to have some background in fact. For example, two common stories focus on why Mullah Omar turned his *madrasa,* or Islamic school, into an armed militia. The first story claims that two young Muslim girls had been kidnapped and raped by bandits, and he sought to avenge this crime; the other is that two young men got into a tank battle in the middle of Qandahar over someone they each wished to rape, and Mullah Omar rescued the intended victim and executed the two men. Taliban supporters generally add that Omar had a vision in which Muhammad commanded him to step forward to restore order and morality.

Details about Mullah Omar's life are sketchy and contested. It is generally accepted that he was born into a poor family either in Qandahar or in the province of Uruzgan in approximately 1962. It is also known that he studied in several Islamic schools in Pakistan but never completed all the work required to officially be a mullah; however, the title is used nevertheless as a sign of respect. Omar fought against the Soviets, and in the process he lost an eye and had the lid sewn shut, a symbol, supporters say, of his willingness to sacrifice personally for his beliefs. There are also reports that one of his wives is a daughter of Osama bin Laden, but the Taliban denies this.

controlled limited areas, mostly by terror and force, none was in a position to exert sufficient national influence to challenge the government, and indeed, most did not intend to do so. They were more than happy to control roads and checkpoints where they could either rob vehicles carrying arms, drugs, or consumer goods or exact huge tolls to allow them to pass.

In the south of Afghanistan, the situation seemed on the verge of change in 1994 with the founding of an Islamic fundamentalist student group. Made up of Pashtuns from the area around Qandahar, the group called themselves the Taliban, taking their name from the word "talib," meaning a seeker of religious knowledge. The Taliban was created by a charismatic local mullah, or religious teacher, named Mohammad Omar. In 1994, Mullah Omar organized his students and others into a militia to fight against what he perceived as the moral chaos of the country, symbolized by both the renegade mujahideen and the government itself. His early successes prompted the Pakistani government to hire the Taliban to protect Pakistani military trucks crossing the country. From the beginning, the Taliban was well financed by Saudi Arabia and Pakistan because of complex motives tied to desires to see Afghanistan stabilized and friendly, but not too independent or powerful.

After the Taliban was asked by the local leadership of Qandahar to bring order to the city, Mullah Omar began to be seen as someone who might be able to restore order throughout the country. Even the United States recognized his potential by sending its ambassador to Pakistan, John Monjo, to pay Mullah Omar a visit in Qandahar in 1994. Mullah Omar was quickly able to add large stretches of southwest Afghanistan to his political base with little bloodshed or violence. He did this by sending individuals into new areas in advance to explain the Taliban's ideas for the country and to ask for people's support. According to scholars Ralph H. Magnus and Eden Naby, "The Taliban program was simple but astonishingly effective. They promised to end the fighting and to restore law and order under the shari'a [Islamic law]. 'Bad' commanders who had taken advantage of their position to enrich themselves were removed, but 'good' commanders who were loyal to Islamic values were confirmed in office."[8]

THE FALL OF RABBANI

With a solid base in the southwest, the Taliban began moving toward Kabul. Ghazni province came under its control early in 1994, as did a suburb south of Kabul that had been the center of operations of Rabbani's chief opponent, Hekmatyar. This created a difficult situation for the Rabbani government in Kabul. Although grateful that Hekmatyar had been driven out of the Kabul area, it realized that the Taliban was now a real threat to its own hold on power.

Rabbani had other problems. Many countries, including the United States, had closed their embassies and refused to recognize his government as legitimate because it had taken power without an open election. At this point, many in the outside world looked upon the Taliban favorably. It had positioned itself as the moral authority the nation seemed to need, and its claims to be committed to democracy gained it a great deal of international support. According to Ralph Magnus and Eden

Naby, when the United Nations asked the Taliban to speak as a national party for Afghanistan, it declined, stating its "willingness to support any government that was achieved through the consensus of the political leaders and represented the will of the people."[9] One top-ranking American official drew a polite but clear contrast between the Taliban and the Rabbani government, praising the Taliban for being unlike "factional leaders . . . reluctant to relinquish their personal power for the overall good of Afghanistan,"[10] a reference to Rabbani's refusal to give in to international and internal pressure to resign.

When Rabbani's government was embarrassed in 1995 by undeniable evidence that it was secretly taking monetary and military support from the Russians to enable it to stay in power, the tide turned decidedly against it. Ironically, it was not clear until later how extensive foreign financial support had been for almost every group that had fought in Afghanistan over the past few decades, including the anti-Communist mujahideen, who had secretly been given billions of dollars by the United States. After Rabbani's secrets had been exposed, the Taliban, which previously had been unable to capture the city of Herat because of the superior military force of the government, was easily able to fan anti-Russian sentiments to march on the city and take control of it in late 1995. But the big prize, Kabul, still awaited. Rabbani desperately tried to put together a coalition that would enable him to stay in power, but he found that although there was support for a coalition government, the main condition for cooperation was that he resign first.

Eventually, Hekmatyar and Rabbani saw that, to prevent the Taliban from taking over the country and putting an end to both their political careers, they would have to reconcile. Hekmatyar became prime minister early in 1996, while Rabbani remained president. But it was too late. The Taliban launched a successful offensive to take Jalalabad and finally reached Kabul in September. Casualties were low in both of the campaigns because there was little resistance. Kabul fell almost without a struggle despite the fact that thirty thousand soldiers were supposed to defend it. Rabbani and Hekmatyar fled north.

THE TALIBAN TAKES POWER

Although the Rabbani government never actually dissolved, the Taliban was effectively the new government of most of Afghanistan by the end of 1996. It controlled the capital, had

forced the last government to flee, and was the undisputed ruler of about two-thirds of the country. However, resistance to the Taliban had been taking shape since its beginnings. In the words of Mullah Omar, his job as leader was to accomplish "the implementation of Islamic order,"[11] to create a country united and ruled by a strict interpretation of Islamic law. Although commitment to Islam ran deep throughout the country, many people did not approve of extremist leaders of any type, religious or not, who limited individual freedom and exacted harsh punishments for dissent.

Areas in the north, such as Mazar-e Sharif, continued to resist the Taliban to a large degree because they did not trust the Pashtuns, who they thought were bent on "imposing a backward-minded Pashtun dictatorship over the ethnic mosaic of Afghanistan."[12] Mazar-e Sharif was a holdout under leaders Abdul Rashid Dostum and Abdul Malik, and the area northeast of Kabul also resisted under Tajik leader Ahmed Shah Masood. Mazar-e Sharif finally came under Taliban control in 1998, but pockets of resistance remained in the 90 percent of

Effectively taking control of Afghanistan by force, Taliban soldiers crowd atop a tank.

the country that was eventually controlled by the Taliban. It was necessary to suppress dissent by violence and terror. The Hazara, considered infidels because they are Shiite rather than Sunni Muslims, were treated particularly severely.

OPPOSITION GROWS

Like the Rabbani government before it, the Taliban was never officially acknowledged by most of the world as the legitimate government of Afghanistan because it had come to power by armed force rather than by the free choice of the people. But legitimate or not, the Taliban soon had a crushing level of control over the people of Afghanistan. It quickly moved to implement its version of shari'a, or Islamic law, declaring that women appearing in public had to be covered from head to toe, with only their hands allowed to remain visible. Furthermore, they would not be permitted to work, or even to be outside their home at all without a male relative accompanying them. Men were required to grow beards eight centimeters in length, long enough to be clutched in a closed hand. Everyone in the workplace was forced to stop for prayer. Movie houses were closed and television was banned. Transgressions of regulations were punishable by beatings or worse. Male heads of households were often beaten, along with a wife or child who had broken a rule, as a way of shaming them for not controlling their families.

Daily life became miserable for everyone except those who felt they were saving the country and bringing it into accord with the will of Allah. The standard of living, already low, was falling, and fewer and fewer people seemed to think their suffering was leading toward any positive result. Most Afghans went along only because they had no choice, but the opposition, led by Masood, Dostum, and others, was well funded from outside sources and had a growing number of willing soldiers.

By 1999, worldwide opposition to the Taliban had escalated, especially in regard to its hostile and inhumane treatment of women and its support of international terrorist groups. After several terrorist attacks around the world, the United Nations put sanctions in place against Afghanistan for the Taliban's support of Osama bin Laden and his organization, al-Qaeda. The Taliban appeared to be willing to try to improve its image, including participating in negotiations for sharing power with Masood, who had emerged as the preeminent leader of opposition forces. These negotiations quickly broke down, as did several

WOMEN UNDER THE TALIBAN

The years of Taliban control were brutal ones for all Afghans, but conditions for women were the harshest of all. Severe restrictions were put on their activities, and failure to comply would subject a woman (and sometimes her husband as well) to brutal beatings on the spot, imprisonment, or even execution. Among the regulations were the following:

• Drivers of any kind of motor vehicle could not give rides to women.

• Women could not work outside the home, unless they were deemed a necessary hospital or clinic worker, and then they had to be segregated from male colleagues.

• Girls could not attend school, and those caught trying to educate them informally were subject to imprisonment.

• Women were not permitted to go out in public except accompanied by a male relative.

• Women who went out in public were required to wear a burkah, a gown that covers the body from head to toe, leaving only the hands visible.

• Women were prohibited from laughing loudly or making noise when they walked.

Many Muslim cultures have traditions and practices that restrict what women can do and require them to cover themselves to varying degrees, but Afghanistan was never in the past viewed as extremist in this regard. The burkah is a particularly difficult constraint for Afghan women. A woven mesh panel over the face enables the woman to see and breathe, but the experience is claustrophobic because it is hard to hear and all peripheral vision is lost. Many Afghans were quick to point out, upon the fall of the Taliban, that they considered the burkah and other such restrictions against women not only un-Afghan but also un-Islamic.

Afghan women under Taliban rule were forced to wear clothing covering their entire bodies.

other similar attempts by the United Nations over the next year. Former king Zahir Shah, from his home in exile near Rome, was asked to draw up a peace plan in early 2001, but the Taliban rejected it outright.

The regime's extremism was underscored a few weeks later, on March 1, 2001, when it blew up the ancient giant stone Buddhas, among the oldest in the world, near Bamian. Mullah Omar called this act simply "breaking stones."[13] The Taliban also destroyed precious artifacts in the Kabul Museum and historic sites at Ghazni at the same time. The shocking destruction of the Buddhas and other priceless remnants of the past served as a stark clarification for many around the world that this was a renegade government that felt no obligation to protect anything or anyone under its control.

THE FALL OF THE TALIBAN

By far the deadliest of these missions was the attack on the World Trade Center in New York and the Pentagon in Washington, D.C., on September 11, 2001. Quickly determining it to be the work of al-Qaeda, the U.S. government demanded that Osama bin Laden and other al-Qaeda leaders be turned over for trial. When it became clear that the Taliban would continue to shelter bin Laden, the United States followed through on its threat to go to war against any country whose government harbored international terrorists. A bombing campaign focused on al-Qaeda and Taliban strongholds and hiding places began on October 7, 2001. By the end of 2001, the Taliban government had been toppled from power, and al-Qaeda had retreated to what seemed to be its last base in Afghanistan, in the Tora Bora Hills near Jalalabad.

A number of important Taliban and al-Qaeda leaders were killed or captured, including key lieutenants to Mullah Omar and Osama bin Laden. However, Omar and bin Laden both eluded death or capture during the bombardment and invasion by the U.S. armed forces, perhaps by crossing the border into Pakistan. Even though they escaped, the Taliban era was over. A coalition government headed by Hamid Karzai, backed by a multinational peacekeeping force, took power, in late December 2001. Its mission during its six-month duration was to put together a functioning government and plan and carry out national elections. However, by early 2002, the coalition's efforts were already being undermined by some warlords who

Osama bin Laden and al-Qaeda

Osama bin Laden was born in Riyadh, Saudi Arabia, in 1957. He was the seventeenth of the fifty-two children of one of the wealthiest men in Saudi Arabia, Muhammad bin Laden, the founder of a major construction company. Bin Laden earned a degree in civil engineering from King Abdul Aziz University in Jedda, Saudi Arabia, in 1979, then left to fight with the mujahideen in the Afghan war against the Soviets. There, he organized a group called al-Qaeda, or "the base," dedicated to the overthrow of the United States and its allies. Bin Laden returned to Saudi Arabia but was forced to leave in 1991 because of his opposition to the Saudi monarchy's alliance with the United States during the Persian Gulf War.

Taking advantage of Sudan's willingness to allow any Muslim to come settle in the country, bin Laden moved to Sudan with a plan to bring terrorists together for training. As a cover, he set up legitimate businesses there, including a tannery, two farms, and a construction business, while continuing to fund al-Qaeda training camps largely out of his personal fortune. In 1996, Sudan expelled him under pressure from the United States, but by then he had already moved much of his operation to Yemen and Afghanistan. Many terrorist attacks, including the 1993 bombing at the World Trade Center, bombings of U.S. embassies and military bases abroad, and various assassination attempts, have now been linked to bin Laden's operations during these early years.

When the U.S. embassies in Kenya and Tanzania were bombed in 1998, the United States retaliated by bombing al-Qaeda training sites in Afghanistan.

Thus, the early stages of a concerted effort against Osama bin Laden, al-Qaeda, and world terrorism began. It was not until the bombing of the naval vessel the USS *Cole* on October 12, 2000, followed by attacks on the World Trade Center and the Pentagon eleven months later, that the war on terrorism was officially announced. A military campaign was initiated in Afghanistan to destroy al-Qaeda and those who supported it, including the Taliban and bin Laden himself.

Saudi Arabian–born terrorist Osama bin Laden.

Hamid Karzai gives a speech to the Afghan people after accepting the role of interim leader of the country.

continued to hold power in their regions by armed force and were proving unreliable at tracking down and turning over remaining Taliban and al-Qaeda leaders. Still, Hamid Karzai's government, with strong worldwide support, had taken the first steps to put the country on more solid social, economic, and political footing after the devastation of the last few decades of anarchy and oppression.

LIFE IN TODAY'S AFGHANISTAN

5

The answer to the question "How do Afghans live?" is an extremely complex one. To begin with, the ethnic diversity of the country makes no one single answer possible. In addition, life in rural Afghanistan is very different from that in Kabul or the other major cities. But perhaps the biggest complication is the fact that, for several decades now, warfare has disrupted life so much that any description of Afghan lifestyles must include both the way people traditionally live and the way they have been forced to live by recent circumstances. Foods they traditionally eat, for example, may have been replaced by supplies provided by foreign countries. What they actually eat, therefore, and what they would eat if given the choice are different, but both are part of their lives and identities.

Regardless of present circumstances, however, several central facts remain the same. The first of these constants is that the country is poor in the best of times, and though things have clearly gotten worse in recent years, the Afghan people are well acquainted with hardship. They are also well acquainted with violence, the second constant in their culture. The third constant, and the one with which any discussion of Afghan culture and life must begin, is the religion that unifies the country, Islam. Although any discussion of life in Afghanistan cannot accurately represent all the important details of each Afghan's lifestyle, these three things are shared by all.

LIVING BY THE QUR'AN

The ways people practice Islam in Afghanistan vary widely and can cause conflict, but the central place of Islam in their lives is unquestionable. Islam is, at its core, an uncomplicated religion to practice. Anyone who accepts the Muslim holy book, the Qur'an, as the word of God, who follows the five pillars of faith, and who lives his or her life in submission to Allah is a Muslim.

THE DEOBANDI *MADRASAS*

Many Afghans found their way to refugee camps in the border regions of Pakistan during the political upheaval of the past few decades. Those who received schooling generally attended what are known as Deobandi *madrasas.* These schools have their roots in the small Indian town of Deoband, near Delhi. In 1867, out of concern that the Western-style education promoted by the British would destroy Islamic culture, religious leaders set up a school there to teach Muslim children the Qur'an and a strict code of personal behavior. In the early twentieth century, many Deobandi *madrasas* were set up near the Afghan border. They grew in importance as the flood of Afghan refugees increased in the 1980s and 1990s. The Deobandi *madrasas* were meant to educate the poor, and their curriculum was limited to the Qur'an, which the students were expected to memorize. Out of one particular *madrasa,* the Darul Uloom Haqqania, near Peshawar, came many of the leaders of the Taliban.

Pankaj Mishra, writing about a recent visit to a *madrasa* in an article in the *New York Review of Books* titled "The Making of Afghanistan," describes the "peeling paint, dust-clogged stairs, broken chairs, unfinished buildings bristling with rusted iron girders, and shabbily clad students . . . with curious fresh faces under elegant white caps." In the kitchen, "flies hovered over the stagnant yellow curry in exposed drains and the freshly chopped mutton on a wide wooden table." But, Mishra points out, "food and lodging were free . . . and the orphans and sons of poor Pashtuns in the refugee camps . . . wouldn't have had many options. Living amid deprivation and squalor, and educated only in a severe ideology [they] developed fast the fantasies of the pure Islamic order" they would bring to their country. The *madrasas* were where many of today's Afghans formed negative opinions about the outside world, including the United States. The *madrasas* continue to operate in a similar fashion, molding the thinking of today's young people.

The five pillars of faith are straightforward and easy to comprehend. Following the Qur'an, however, is a more complex matter, because there is controversy over what it actually says. The Qur'an is always recited and read in Arabic, but most Afghans are not literate even in Dari or Pashto, the two main languages of Afghanistan, much less in Arabic. As a result, they must rely on mullahs to interpret the Qur'an for them. This makes religious leaders extremely important since Muslims believe that following the Qur'an is essential to please Allah and earn a place in paradise. Over time, this reliance on religious leaders who may be only semiliterate themselves and simply pass on what their predecessors taught them has resulted in widely varying and conflicting practices. Each group, however, is convinced that the practices they were taught adhere closely to the Qur'an. Conversely, they often see the practices of others as un-Muslim and treat them as enemies or, at the very least, inferiors.

Regional and ethnic differences in the interpretation of the Qur'an are an important factor in the overall culture of Afghanistan. However, in recent years a movement generally referred to as Islamism has entered the picture. Islamists are people who politicize Islam, meaning that they favor using Islam as the foundation for systems of law and government. Typically, Islamists support shari'a, believing that mullahs can find, in the Qur'an, the answers to legal, social, and political questions. The Taliban leadership was a council of Islamist mullahs who subjected the people of Afghanistan to many new restrictions and requirements they claimed were required by the Qur'an.

Punishment for anything considered an infraction of shari'a was severe and swift. Failing to pray at the prescribed times was punishable by imprisonment. Music, other than religious chanting, was prohibited in public places and even at private family celebrations. Even hobbies considered useless, such as kite flying, were banned. Photos and paintings depicting people were ordered destroyed as a form of worship of false images. Restrictions against women left them almost entirely housebound and subject to violence at the hands of men. Taliban police officers had the authority to beat anyone they saw breaking even the smallest of regulations, and those who were imprisoned had no protections or rights.

CITY LIFE UNDER THE TALIBAN

Clearly, such restrictions had a profound effect on daily life. This was particularly true in the cities, where people could be watched more closely. Police checkpoints were set up along city streets, and a curfew was strictly enforced. The overall climate of violence and repression of the past few decades had made it easy for the police to shoot first and ask questions later or never. Afghans knew that something as simple as a trip to the market could involve perilous encounters with police, whose job was not to ensure a smooth functioning and peaceful society, but to sniff out and punish transgressions of Talibanic law.

The restrictions on women made it difficult for them to tend to their homes and families, because they could not easily shop or run errands. Most schools closed because teachers were traditionally women, and they could no longer work. Women had been an important part of the workforce during the Marxist era, and many businesses suffered when women could no longer come to their jobs. It also became more difficult for women to keep their families clean and healthy. Bathing facilities are generally absent in most homes, and the public baths on which people relied, already carefully segregated by gender, were closed by the Taliban altogether. The Qur'an, the mullahs said, forbade any public display of nakedness.

Adding to the difficulties of life in the cities were the destruction stemming from the civil war before the rise of the Taliban and the ongoing struggle of resistance movements against the Taliban. Well-armed militias fought against each other so often that city streets were soon pocked with craters, and buildings were bombed and burned out. However, despite the destruction, life did go on. People still congregated at the marketplaces, attended prayers in the mosques, and ran their businesses. In fact, it became a source of pride not even to flinch or run at the sound of an approaching mortar shell. When someone was killed or injured by a bomb or police, the air would briefly be filled with yelling and screaming. The body would then be quickly removed and normal traffic would resume, often simply going around the new patch of blood or crater in the street.

RURAL LIFE IN WARTIME

In the countryside, between outbreaks of violence, life continued to consist, in the words of journalist Sarah Boxer, of "fishing, game playing, planting, herding, buying and selling, and praying." [14] In fact, according to author Pankaj Mishra, the most remote villages only became aware of the Taliban when Toyota pickups filled with "young turbaned men and guns crammed in the back" created "new sources of fear." [15] Some areas, however, have been seriously impacted by the prolonged warfare between the militias of rival leaders. Villages known to be strongholds of one group or another have been shelled or bombed, and many of their people maimed and killed. In addition, the mountain passes that many rural Afghans depend on to reach the markets where they sell their products and buy supplies inevitably become danger zones in times of strife. Trigger-happy soldiers and highway robbers patrolling the

roads have made life unsafe and frightening everywhere in the country.

Those who live in the steppes have been more deeply affected by civil war and by the repression of the Taliban because the location of their communities made them more accessible than those in the mountains. Once a town or village became contested by rival militias or was suspected of harboring enemies, it generally was only a matter of time before it was reduced to rubble and its people were killed or fled to join the millions of other refugees made homeless by the years of strife. Nomads of the deserts and other regions have, in some respects, suffered less because they have no permanent communities to destroy, but they have been particularly hard hit by the indiscriminate placing of land mines over much of the countryside. Clearly, no one has escaped the negative impact of years of war and lawlessness in Afghanistan.

Heavily armed Taliban militiamen ride in the back of pickup trucks at a rally in Kabul.

LIFE'S PASSAGES
Still, in the cities and villages of the desert, steppes, and mountains, life follows traditional patterns based on the seasons and

THE CALL TO PRAYER

Jason Elliot, a British journalist who has lived and traveled exten-
sively in Afghanistan, says in his book *An Unexpected Light,* that "traditionally at
least, the act of worship is so finely woven into the fabric of life that . . . even in
the extremity of war, [it] is as unobtrusive as the motion of the sun. . . . Often in
Kabul I have been in a taxi when the driver has politely asked if I wouldn't mind
waiting while he attended the midday prayers. I have been on buses, too, where
the driver pulls over near a stream or well to let the passengers pray." A ritual
cleansing with water precedes the prayer, although dry soil can be used if water
is not available. Elliot tells of watching men in warfare "unslinging their rifles
and patting their hands into the dust at their feet" as a prelude to prayer. "In the
countryside one sees people at prayer on their rooftops, in their dusty court-
yards, in fields and on mountaintops; the sight of a solitary farmer, who, after
the day's toil spreads his pattu [prayer rug] to begin his devotions, is one by
which only the most hard-hearted can fail to be moved."

The prayers always begin with these words, called out in Arabic by the prayer
leader, or said softly by the individual:

Praise be to God, Lord of the two worlds

The most merciful and most forgiving

Lord of the Day of Judgment

It is you we adore and in Whom we seek help

Guide us along the straight path. . . .

Much of the ritual, including physical gestures such as touching the
forehead to the ground to symbolize
the equality of all before God, is the
same each time, but at some points
the worshiper is free to choose
verses of the Qur'an he or she
wishes to recite. The overall effect, in
the words of Jason Elliot, is to
"loosen the noose of the world that
tightens around the soul in the
course of the day and redirect the
thoughts and feeling toward the Divine."

*An Afghan man reads from the
Qur'an during his midday prayer.*

the important passages in life. Although the excitement of a birth, wedding, or funeral may completely take over life in a village in a way it does not in a city with varied activities and more hectic rhythms, city dwellers generally remember and treasure their rural roots. Even in the bustling neighborhoods of Kabul, people carry on many of the age-old rituals of their ancestors. The different lifestyle of the cities, however, as well as exposure to other people's ways, often weakens the desire, especially among new generations, to stick to traditional practices. Nevertheless, historians and sociologists agree that traditions are an important way the spirit and identity of a people are kept alive through times of hardship. Despite whatever else is going on in their lives, Afghans of each ethnic group have generally held fast to those practices that bind them together and create a sense of continuity with the past and belief in the future.

Regardless of ethnic group, pregnancy and birth are generally accompanied by numerous ceremonies. According to Sirdar Ikbal Ali Shah, "even before he enters the world, the Afghan makes a stir." [16] Hospital or doctor-assisted births are rare, and most Afghan babies are born at home with the help of midwives, who are usually female neighbors or relatives with no medical training. Male relatives commonly wait outside the house and shoot off rifles, beat drums, shout, and otherwise make as much noise as possible when the birth is announced, to scare away evil spirits. The baby is wrapped in a special cloth embroidered with verses from the Qur'an, and soon after the birth, a mullah whispers in the baby's ear the words of the prayer used to call the faithful to worship. This act is similar to baptism for Christians, and is believed to give the child his or her faith. In some ethnic groups, babies are not named for six months, at which time a special ceremony is held for that purpose.

When a person dies, it is particularly important in most groups that traditions be carefully followed. Special verses from the Qur'an are recited, and the body is washed and wrapped in a shroud in accordance with the customs of each particular group. The grave must be dug so that the dead person's head is pointing toward Mecca, the holy center of the Muslim faith. Among some Pashtuns, the dimensions of the grave are also of critical importance. Boards are placed two feet above the upper part of the body in keeping with the Muslim belief that on Judgment Day a horn will sound and the dead will be raised

Afghan men pray over the body of a young man wrapped in a shroud. He was killed by a cluster bomb in the U.S. strikes.

from their graves. The two-foot clearance will enable the dead person to sit up. In some ethnic groups, no heavy materials, such as gravestones, are used because it may make it more difficult for the body to escape the grave on Judgment Day.

Weddings usually involve the most elaborate ceremonies of all, especially in groups that practice purdah, the custom of keeping women secluded inside the home, away from all contact with men outside their family. Like the various forms of veiling practiced in Muslim countries, purdah is felt to be a means of protecting the purity of women in a world where men's actions and instincts dominate. In these very conservative groups, young men and women have no way to meet, so marriages must be arranged between their families. This task is difficult because no one in the potential groom's family has precise knowledge of what potential brides exist in their community. Families in some Pashtun groups begin in their son's late teens to find him a suitable bride, a process that will take several years. They hire a woman as a secret scout, and she socializes with the families presumed to have marriageable daughters. She reports back about their habits and finances, as well as the health, manners, and physical appearance of potential brides.

When a suitable bride is chosen, the groom's family will make casual social calls and offer gifts, sometimes for several years, but no references will be made to the possibility of marriage. Even when the subject is eventually raised, it is done vaguely. The length of this process is reflected in an Afghan saying that consent is not given until the soles of the young man's family's shoes are as thin as an onion skin from all the visits to the young woman's house. The betrothal is made official by a lengthy process involving special ceremonies, prayers, and foods. The wedding cannot take place often for as long as a year because there are so many ceremonial tasks to be carried out and so much work to be done to prepare the new couple's wardrobe, home, and necessary supplies. The wedding is a several-day process in which the bride and groom do not meet until well into the celebration; their first glimpse of each other is through a strategically placed mirror. The wedding is followed by a period of visitations to new family members and then eventually settling down, usually in the groom's family's home, to which rooms may have been added to house them.

Afghan women surround a smiling bride in one of the many ceremonies leading up to the wedding.

REESTABLISHING NORMALCY

Such elaborate traditions can only be fully maintained when life is not disrupted by war. This has not been the case for the millions of Afghans who have been forced from their homes by violence, hunger, or political oppression and now live outside their country. Afghan immigrant communities exist around the world. However, the typical immigrant lives in desperate poverty in one of many refugee camps just across the border in Pakistan. Afghan refugees live without adequate means of keeping themselves clean, with poor diets, and with minimal shelter. Many Afghan refugees' memories include horrible images of death and destruction, followed by uprooting and resettlement in a strange land. Those born in the camps have no other memories, and their identity as Afghans, or as members of specific ethnic groups, has been kept alive only by the efforts of older refugees.

Despite all the suffering of its people, and its historical lack of peace, Afghanistan has not been a place where hatred and negativity have dominated hearts and spirits. Today, peace and a better future are desperately wanted. "We don't want your guns," an orphan working as a waiter in Kabul said recently. "We want your help. The world has given us nothing but death." [17] Whether the experiences of the newest generations have changed Afghans forever, or whether older ways will reassert themselves now that it appears to be safe for people to return to their regions and to their old styles of life, remains to be seen. However, there is no doubt that daily life will bear the scars of decades of oppression and violence in the minds and on the bodies of Afghans for many years to come.

The Crossroads of Art and Culture

6

One of the basic principles of human life is that essential needs must be met before people can concentrate on anything else. People look for food and shelter first, and only when their basic survival seems at least temporarily assured will they turn their attention to more abstract things such as the pursuit of beauty. In war-torn and desperately poor countries like Afghanistan, simply living from one day to the next presents constant challenges, so it should come as no surprise that there are few occasions to produce or appreciate art in its various forms.

Added to this situation is the hostility that the Taliban showed toward most art forms. Movie houses were closed, all music except religious chanting was banned, and many priceless artifacts of the past were deliberately destroyed. In this climate, many musicians, visual artists, and other creative people put their work on hold or continued to work only in deepest secrecy. Many others fled to neighboring countries such as Iran and Pakistan, or to Europe, Canada, Australia, and the United States.

From this, one might conclude that Afghan art and culture is in a serious state of decline, but this is not in fact true. Within Afghanistan itself, there are still many reminders of the unique culture, such as traditional dress and celebration of holidays, and in remote areas beyond the daily reach of the Taliban, cultural life has continued largely unchanged. In the marketplace, art forms such as weaving rugs and cloth have continued to flourish because they are sources of income for many people. Only "un-Islamic" or Western-influenced art such as films, most music, and paintings of the human figure were vigorously suppressed.

Beauty has continued to spring up within Afghanistan despite the dust and debris of civil war and the choking effect of

*A woman weaves a rug,
a craft that Afghanistan
is noted for around the
world.*

religious extremism. However, many creative people chose instead to leave their country over the past few decades to pursue their art in a freer and more supportive environment. In fact, preserving and developing Afghan artistic expression has become a mission for many Afghans living abroad. There are a number of online magazines and websites either devoted exclusively to Afghan art and culture or featuring it prominently. There are also dozens of lovingly tended web pages and smaller websites kept by individuals who post articles, links, and other information about their special interests such as contemporary Afghan art and music. A brief online search will yield a dozen or more sites providing Afghan music of all varieties. Traditional arts have been preserved and new ideas have been expressed over the last few decades, whether by an expatriate at a keyboard in Sydney, Australia, or a veiled woman at her loom in Kabul.

MUSIC

According to journalist Sarah Boxer, "The music of Afghanistan is deeply rooted in tradition and folklore, and it is very much alive in the hearts of the people. It is an essential part of their life, and a colorful expression of the national temperament." [18]

The instruments used in traditional music today date back four thousand years ago to the ancient kingdom of Ariana, one of the names by which Afghanistan used to be known. The *toula* is a flute still used today, derived from the ancient *dandweehi*. The *toula* is said to have been introduced to China in the era of overland trade, beginning a major art form in that country. It is decorated with colored paint and is played pointing down like a clarinet. According to writer Nabi Kohzad, "it is said that the ancient mountain passes and valleys of Afghanistan were once filled with tunes . . . and if you listen to the wind at night in an Afghan valley you can hear the ancient, harmonious melodies played out in the breezes that blow." [19]

The oldest Afghan string instrument is known as a *tar*. In its most basic and ancient version, it has two strings. The names of more modern instruments such as the Indian sitar, Afghan *dutar*, and Western guitar have their root in the ancient name "tar" and are derived from this ancient Afghan instrument. The *dutar* was developed in Herat in 1965 by a musician who wanted to duplicate the sounds of the extremely complex instrument the *rubab*. The *rubab* is an eighteenth-century instrument commonly used today as a solo instrument or as an accompaniment

Men and boys crowd around musical instruments, playing late into the night. Music was once again allowed after the Taliban was defeated.

to singing. The *rubab* is itself a descendant of the *robab*, from which first the medieval lute and then the violin and cello are thought to derive. The *robab* is also still played today; it consists of four gut strings sounded with a pick called a plectrum, and contains a number of other vibrating or "sympathetic" strings.

Two types of drums are also an important part of Afghan music. The first is a pair of small, connected drums, an example of which is the *dhol*. The second is a single drum known as the *dowl* or the *zerbaghali*. These usually bulge slightly in the middle and are smaller at the base, like a water goblet. Afghan music also makes use of a small, keyed Persian instrument similar to a dulcimer, an accordion-like harmonium, and the clarinet.

Musical styles have traditionally been quite different from region to region, with the two most important styles originating in Herat and Kabul. Herati music is known for the liveliness of its melodies and has a heritage dating back to the Timurid dynasty, when Herat was a cultural hub in Central Asia. The music of Kabul has a strong similarity to Indian music in its vocal style, its instrumentation, and the composition of its pieces. Indian-influenced Afghan music is structured very differently than that of the West. It lacks conventional Western melodies, rhythms, and harmonies and has a style of singing that is very nasal and fluid.

In recent years, increased contact between different Afghan ethnic groups has resulted in some blending of styles, and Uzbeki, Tajiki, and other musical traditions have added to the richness of Afghan traditional music. But Western technology, instruments, and styles have had by far the most profound influence on Afghan music today. Musicians, however, generally update traditional styles rather than abandon them entirely, incorporating electric guitars, synthesizers, organs, and other Western instruments and employing the latest technology to mix and orchestrate their music.

DECORATIVE ARTS

Openness to the use of whatever materials or technologies are available is the hallmark of other Afghan artists as well. Because so many Afghans are nomadic or seminomadic, art forms that are easily portable, such as jewelry and woven cloth, have been favored. Because the country is poor, precious materials such as gold and gems are generally seen only in small quantities as accents in their art. The emphasis, instead, has been on the

SAVING AFGHANS' ARTISTIC HERITAGE

During the nineteenth century, Great Britain and other colonial powers removed many of the art treasures and antiquities from the areas they colonized for display in museums in their own countries. By the middle of the twentieth century, attitudes had changed considerably, and countries not only resisted further removals but also demanded the return of many items that they considered to be stolen by their occupiers. Though most countries have had limited success in getting any items back, the art world and organizations such as the United Nations have taken firm stands against removing any item of cultural significance from its country of origin. Today, this applies primarily to smugglers and unethical dealers who still look for tombs to rob and inadequately guarded museums to burglarize, but the ban extends even to aboveboard museum purchases.

For the last twenty years, many Afghans have pleaded for the United Nations Educational, Scientific, and Cultural Organization (UNESCO) to reverse its policy and assist with removing the art treasures of Afghanistan for safekeeping in light of massive looting and sales on the black market. Many treasures have also been broken up to sell in pieces or otherwise damaged by treasure hunters with no sense of the value of these irreplaceable objects. A museum set up in Switzerland by an Afghan-run foundation took a first step in 2000 by serving as a temporary home for art that had been rescued or returned by ethical collectors who didn't know they had purchased stolen property. Despite the clear need, UNESCO was unwilling to change its policy until the spring of 2001, when the blowing up of the Buddhas at Bamian and the Taliban's indifference to safeguarding the Kabul museum and other collections made it clear that not to act was to assist in cultural destruction. However, the procedures for actually coming into a country and confiscating its treasures, and the difficult politics behind doing so, kept the project from really getting under way. Now that the Taliban has fallen, art and culture lovers around the world hope that, with adequate safeguards against looters, the crisis has now passed. There are even plans by private parties to rebuild the Buddhas at Bamian.

beauty that skilled hands and eyes can bring to simple materials, and Afghanistan has achieved wide renown for centuries for the quality of its weaving, embroidery, jewelry, and other decorative arts.

In past centuries, Afghanistan, like other Muslim countries, was renowned for small and exquisitely crafted and detailed art forms such as illuminated (hand-painted) books and miniature paintings. Fifteenth-century artist Behzad of Herat is one of the finest miniaturists of the medieval era. He painted detailed landscapes and scenes of rural life in the space of only a few square inches. This emphasis on the small but exquisite has characterized Afghan art for several millennia, and it can still be seen in the artistic creations of every region in the country, from the smallest village to the largest cities.

Today, Afghan decorative arts tend to fall into two broad categories: clothing, and household items such as rugs and decorated kitchenware. Styles vary by ethnic group and by region. Some designs are so individual and precise that it is possible to identify the village in which the item was made. As in all Islamic countries, designs tend to be based on geometric patterns ranging from bold and brightly colored diamond shapes decorating a blanket to intricate beaded fringe on the hem of a skirt. Ceremonial costumes such as those worn for weddings often take months of painstaking work to decorate, and when finished they may include dye work, beadwork, woven ribbon, tassels, embroidery, and patchwork all on the same garment— a true feast for the senses. In fact, young girls are taught that the quality of their embroidery and other detailed work will help them be marriageable, and girls as young as eight can already turn out professional-quality work.

Some clothing is made for specific purposes. Many Afghan ethnic groups, for example, commonly give silk head cloths, to be wrapped into turbans worn in different styles, as gifts on important occasions. However, much of the decoration on clothing is simply meant to add beauty to items that are worn daily. Because many Afghans are superstitious, they often will include designs thought to ward off the evil eye or keep malicious jinn (genies) at bay. For example, a ribbon, pin, or other item with a symbolic design will often be placed over the blankets or cloths in which babies are wrapped.

During more peaceful times, Afghanistan had a number of flourishing cottage industries based on decorative arts. Embroidered sheepskin coats and woven blankets (called afghans in the West) were valuable exports. But the most prized items of all are weavings, primarily rugs, which feature intricate designs colored with bright natural dyes. These rugs provide a source of income for many Afghans, but their origins are based in their daily needs. Many Afghan homes have dirt floors, and a covering of some sort helps keep dust under control. Also, Muslims use a small prayer rug for their daily devotions, and for many this item is the most precious thing they own. All the talent and inspiration of generations of weavers have gone into making these rugs as beautiful as the finest jewelry.

Jewelry itself is also prized in Afghanistan, particularly among nomadic women who, like their counterparts around the world, tend to wear their entire fortunes as they travel. Men, nomadic and otherwise, usually dress more simply and practically, gaining their status in part from the visible wealth they have been able to provide their wives. Women's ears, noses, necks, wrists, and ankles are adorned with silver and other metals worked into beautiful designs and sometimes accented with small pieces of gemstone, mirror, and other decorations. To see an Afghan woman dressed in her full regalia is to be in the presence of a walking work of art, a living museum of the history and culture of her people.

Afghan rugs, prized items for income and daily needs, are sprawled in the sun to dry after being washed.

VISUAL ARTS

Although the decorative arts are the ones by which Afghanistan is most immediately identified, there are artists, many of them in exile, making contributions to other visual art forms. A number of Afghans have made their marks as internationally known photographers, including Yama Rahimi and Abdullah Qazi. Painter Ustad Mohammad Aziz created watercolors of rural scenes and people in his home city of Kabul. Ustad Mashal was renowned for his contributions to public art in Herat, including murals and statues. He died in exile in 1998, having lived long enough to learn that the Taliban had decapitated his statues of horses and whitewashed his mural in the Herat Bazaar, calling them idolatrous and un-Islamic. Other younger painters have fled to the United States and elsewhere, but have found maintaining careers as artists extremely difficult.

LITERATURE AND FILM

The Afghan film industry is yet another victim of hard times. Once considered to be one of the most potentially interesting and innovative in Central Asia, its directors found it difficult to get funding for anything but propaganda films in the last few decades, and the situation grew worse with the outright ban on filmmaking by the Taliban. Television, also outlawed by the Taliban, has ceased to exist altogether. Radio, however, has continued in a heavily censored format. Afghans are so starved for things to listen to that they often cluster around radios to hear broadcasts in English by the BBC world news service despite the fact that most cannot understand what is being said. When the Taliban fell, Afghan radio stations almost immediately began broadcasting previously forbidden music, and it is likely that Afghan film and television will be revived once studios become operational.

Poets and other Afghan writers have generally been able to continue their work, often from abroad. They have outlets such as the Internet, magazines, and other publishers for their work, and a number of writers have achieved renown as spokespeople for the Afghan experience in exile and for the people they left behind. Poets usually write in either Dari or Pashto, but as yet much of their work is untranslated. Some of the more influential poets of recent decades include Usted Khalilullah Khalili, Abdul Sami Hamed, Ghulan Ahmad Naweed, and Gulam Nabi Ashqari.

NEW HOME, NEW LIFE

More than two decades of war and civil strife have left most Afghans thinking there is very little they would want to hear about on the radio. But three times a week, Afghans, whether still at home or in refugee camps, crowd around any available radio to hear the latest from Upper Village, Lower Village, and Sarband Village. These fictional towns are the setting for *New Home, New Life*, a soap opera that has been on the air since 1993 and aired its one thousandth episode in August 2001. It is so popular that an estimated two out of three Afghans listen to each episode. The story centers around a farmer named Nek Mohammad and other characters such as Nazir, a bumbling night watchman. As with American soap operas, several stories are interwoven, allowing every listener to identify with particular people and situations.

But *New Home, New Life* has a purpose beyond being one of the few forms of entertainment not banned as idolatry by the Taliban, as television and movies were. Since more than half the population is illiterate and many have little contact with accurate information about health and other important matters, the show is used as a way of delivering essential information. One story line, for instance, might feature a mother worried about a child who is sick with an illness that is common among malnourished people. During the course of the show, she learns how to treat her child. Another story might weave in advice to improve crop yield or cite the advantages of getting immunized. After the events of September 11, 2001, when air strikes were imminent and new waves of Afghans fled toward the camps on the country's borders, the show turned its focus to helping new refugees cope with displacement and prepare for winter in a strange, new place. One recent episode dealt with a refugee family who could not find anyone willing to take in strangers. Nek Mohammad steps in and finds them shelter in a local mosque and then delivers a message about tolerance and the Muslim virtue of hospitality and charity.

New Home, New Life serves an important purpose while entertaining millions, and its stars are so popular that they are mobbed when they make public appearances—even though it is only their voices by which they are known. The characters are so real that on one episode when Nazir tried unsuccessfully to get married, he received hundreds of marriage proposals from families with marriageable daughters or sisters.

These poets and other writers build on a centuries-old tradition of oral storytelling. Those who can tell a story effectively are much appreciated in Afghanistan, for oral recitation of familiar tales is one of the main ways history, ethics, beliefs, and behavior are taught in a society where schooling is sporadic and many people are left illiterate. Written literature also has a long heritage in Afghanistan, dating from the first centuries

THE POETRY OF EXILE

Poetry, because it is one of the chief ways of expressing people's deepest longings and most profound experiences, has generally thrived in times of adversity. For Afghan poets, this has been the case, especially for those who left their country and often harbor complex and even guilty feelings about having done so. The best of these poets are able to capture the feeling of longing to return and the pain at what has happened to their land. Two of these poets, Shabgir Pulliadian and Noozar Elias, are among those who have had some of their work translated into English. The following, quoted in *Afghanradio.com*, is an excerpt of Pulliadian's "Next Year":

Oh my homeland, my ruined land!

I said next year

I would pack up with the friendly spring

to return to your mountain peaks. . . .

I said next year

in the dusty streets I would sit and talk

with orphans who have in their eyes fountains of tears. . . .

Oh land of ruins!

Your flowers are so seared by hands of fire!

Another year has come but where is your spring? . . .

This poem is Noozar Elias's "Thirst," quoted in the October–December 1997 issue of *Lemar-Aftaab:*

A thirst is inside us

the thirst for bold burning deserts

the thirst for scarlet days

the thirst for wild storms.

Our branches—cold.

Our roots—dried up.

Our gardens—gone.

Our bushes—withered.

A thirst is inside us

the thirst of many long years

—many long voiceless years—

a thirst is inside us—ardent.

after the establishment of Islam. The *Shah Nameh* (Book of Kings) is one of these early works, an epic poem consisting of sixty thousand rhymed couplets completed in 1010 by a Persian poet writing in Dari. In the seventeenth century, Kushhal Kattak, a Pashtun warrior poet, wrote works meant to outline proper codes of behavior.

In recent years, some writers have used traditional forms to describe and explain the changes Afghanistan has undergone in the past few decades. The most successful of these authors is Sayyed Burhanuddin Majruh, who in 1972 published several volumes in classical Dari poetic style about exiled travelers who discuss ancient stories in light of modern events. Other writers have favored nonfiction such as sociological and historical works, often stressing Islamic perspectives.

With the increased interest in Afghanistan prompted by U.S. involvement in the region after September 11, 2001, many Afghan intellectuals have found new and eager audiences for their works. Likewise, artists and artisans are likely to find that Westerners, curious about Afghan history and culture, are anxious to support the rebuilding of the country by purchasing the art objects, jewelry, clothing, and other items Afghans will again be able to produce for export. As Afghans emerge from the oppression of the past decades, they will once again be able to enjoy for themselves, and show the world, the beauty of their artistic heritage.

A page from the Shah Nameh *depicts a reception of the king of Kabul in the Palace of Mirhah.*

7

FACING THE FUTURE: CONTEMPORARY CHALLENGES

"Our country, as a result of the long war, had been distracted. We need hard work from all Afghans. We should put our hands together to be brothers and friends. Forget the painful past."[20] When Hamid Karzai, a Pashtun, uttered these words at his inauguration as the new prime minister of an interim government for Afghanistan on December 22, 2001, he was dressed in traditional Uzbek clothing and spoke to the crowd in both official languages of the country, Pashto and Dari. He clearly wanted to show, by his dress and bilingual speech, his commitment to building an Afghanistan in which everyone counted. This was also apparent in the diversity of the twenty-nine-member cabinet attending the ceremony, which consisted of members of all the main ethnic groups, both Sunni and Shiite Muslims, and women as well as men. In a moment well documented by television cameras, when Karzai promised to bring peace to Afghanistan, a room full of warlords brushed tears from their eyes. In the room that day, the desire to have Afghanistan's future be different from its past was clearly strong and widely shared.

Many Afghans from a wide range of ethnic backgrounds and religious orientations, including some who historically have been unable to coexist peaceably, were briefly united at the end of 2001 by the goal of removing the Taliban from power. Their leaders and representatives sat side by side to participate in the historic moment of Karzai's inauguration. However, now that a true national government has been achieved, it is likely to prove difficult to keep Afghans working together. Divisiveness and mutual suspicions run very deep, as does the warlords' tradition of putting their own interests over the good of the larger society. Within a month of Karzai's inauguration, the militias of some of the same warlords who had been at the ceremony had resumed the violence, and new stories surfaced of bombings, shootings, and highway robbery. Further complicating the problem is the devastating effect years of war have had on the educational, environmental, social, and economic condition of the country. This devastation did not stop with the fall of the Taliban, for regions of the country, suspected of harboring terrorists, continued to be

HAMID KARZAI

Hamid Karzai, sworn in as Afghanistan's prime minister in December 2001, has a remarkable blend of characteristics and qualifications that made him an acceptable choice to the diverse and often quarrelsome group charged with coming up with a plan for an interim government after the fall of the Taliban. A Durrani Pashtun, from which all but one of Afghanistan's leaders have been chosen, Karzai is the son of the chief of the Popolzai tribe, one of the most influential within the Durrani itself. Karzai was born on December 24, 1957, in Qandahar, and later went abroad for his college education, where he learned to speak English fluently.

Karzai has a long history of involvement with the tangled politics of Afghanistan. He served as a deputy foreign minister in the first mujahideen government in 1992, and then threw his support behind the Taliban when it became clear the government could not stop the rising anarchy in the country. However, he quickly became disenchanted with the Taliban's extremist views, and when he saw evidence that Pakistanis and other foreigners had infiltrated its leadership, he knew that the Taliban must be stopped before further damage was done to the country. When American air strikes began in Afghanistan in October 2001, Karzai and another Pashtun, Abdul Haq, secretly began organizing resistance from inside Pakistan. Haq was captured and hanged, but U.S. special forces saved Karzai from a similar fate in a daring helicopter rescue. This rescue has caused some concern among Afghans today because it showed that Karzai had very close personal links with the United States, and some people question whether this means he will be independent enough from its influence while serving as prime minister.

However, no one questions Karzai's courage or his commitment to a free and self-governing Afghanistan. He led a group of several thousand fellow Pashtuns in the assault on Qandahar that led to the fall of the Taliban, then showed his statesmanship by his largely successful efforts to negotiate a surrender with minimal bloodshed. Soon after, a coalition government was put together to see Afghanistan through the transition period between the fall of the Taliban and national elections to choose a permanent government. Karzai was selected to be its head, but at his inauguration his father was not in the audience. He was assassinated two years earlier, a murder attributed to the Taliban.

bombed by U.S. forces, and an international peacekeeping force exchanged gunfire with local militias. If and when calm and order can be restored, Afghanistan will have the best chance in decades to build a peaceful and productive society, but the challenges it faces are huge.

BUILDING AN EFFECTIVE GOVERNMENT

The first key element in a stable, peaceful country is a government that has the ability to work through complex problems and put solutions into effect. Though tyrants can keep order at least for a while by force and fear, modern nations understand that democratic institutions, in which the citizens themselves identify the problems and solutions, are the best way to achieve long-term stability. Afghanistan's history has been characterized by wide swings between oppressive central governments and anarchy, giving it little experience with the democratic process. Its current interim government, however, shows a commitment to giving democracy a chance. It includes a Pashtun prime minister; 2 Hazara, 1 Uzbek, and 1 Tajik minister; and 24 additional cabinet members, including 9 Tajik, 2 Hazara, 5 Pashtun, 2

Members of the widely diverse interim government of Afghanistan are sworn in on December 22, 2001.

Uzbek, 1 Nuristani, and 5 Shiite Muslims. Among these officials is Sima Samar, a Hazara woman who heads the Ministry of Women's Affairs, and several female cabinet members.

This structure reflects not only the diversity of the country, but also the challenge ahead in creating unity. Clearly, it will be difficult for twenty-nine very different individuals to reach agreement on important issues affecting the people they represent. However, some interesting dynamics already appear to be in play. Among these is the role of the Pashtuns. Karzai is Pashtun, and his segment of the Pashtun, the Durrani, has produced most of the nation's leaders. Karzai's selection as prime minister rankled some people who felt that a break from the past might be better; others, however, thought that the element of continuity would be good when so much else was changing. As a counterbalance to the Pashtun leadership, the Pashtuns are underrepresented in the cabinet as a whole, in favor of groups that traditionally have had less chance to participate. This is seen as a good sign that a new and more inclusive Afghanistan is on the horizon.

Karzai's desire to be inclusive has led to some difficult but important decisions, including an appointment of General Abdul Rashid Dostum as deputy defense minister. Dostum was a key leader in the Northern Alliance, controlling the Mazar-e Sharif area. Dostum had had difficulty getting along with other opposition leaders, and it was clear that in some respects it would be easier to exclude him from the interim government. Karzai knew, however, that it was essential to bring even quarrelsome parties into the process if long-term acceptance of a unified government was to be achieved. Also, the hope was that cooperation between two powerful military figures, Defense Minister Mohammad Qassem Fahim and Dostum, might lead to the development of a national army and disbanding of independent militias, a necessary element in long-term peace and stability.

The second key element in establishing a stable and peaceful country is a public that accepts the authority of the government. Although the typical Afghan needs no convincing that peace is preferable to interminable civil war, members of the varying warring factions must agree to lay down their arms and allow governmental processes to work. One of Karzai's first steps in this regard was to ask the former king, Zahir Shah, to spearhead the effort to get the Taliban and mujahideen groups to turn in their arms. This program met with early success, but it remains to be seen whether all armed Afghans will follow suit. If they do not, others may rearm themselves for protection. If the thousands of communities, large and small, in the valleys, deserts, and mountains of Afghanistan cannot be kept free of violence, it will not matter a great deal if the government is otherwise functioning smoothly and inclusively, because peace and stability will still elude this land.

THE ROLE OF ISLAM

One of the issues on which there is likely to be difficulty achieving consensus is the role of Islam in the political structure, and to what extent the Qur'an should be used to shape and administer a government. Even though the majority of Afghans deplore the extremes of the Taliban and feel it gave Islam a bad name, many believe there is a significant role for the mullahs and Islamic law at least at the local level. But how a system governing the executive, legislative, and judicial branches of government can function with two very different and potentially contradictory kinds of law remains to be seen. For example, the procedures for trial and punishment for a crime such as burglary might be very different in a city like Kabul than they would be in a remote area where mullahs make most important decisions. It will not work to have a system that overrules the mullahs because people will not accept this kind of government interference with their traditional ways. It also will not work to have every region free to create its own laws and punishments. Both extremes will result in the same kind of disunity that has kept Afghanistan at war internally and vulnerable to intrusions from the outside.

There is no doubt that the interim government will be looking to shape an Islam-centered society. However, it will be difficult to agree on what that means, because the Qur'an is interpreted in so many different ways. For example, there are widely varying interpretations of what the Qur'an actually says about women's rights and roles. During the Soviet era, women had more government support for their individual freedom and their public roles in government, social services, and business than they had in the past. But many today still do not think that was appropriate, and the fall of the Taliban will not bring about widespread freedom for women. Even now, after the fall of the Taliban, many women continue to go veiled in public and try to hide their faces if a man unexpectedly enters a room. Many women are likely to continue to accept men's domination, however brutal and repressive, simply because tradition runs very deep and they do not believe there is any real hope of change. Though they may want more freedom, they are not sure it is safe to exercise it yet. In fact, media reports have described women going veiled to feminist rallies and meetings, removing their veils during the event, then returning veiled to their homes.

WOMEN AND THE QUR'AN

One of the most controversial aspects of Islam today is the treatment of women in Muslim societies. Even within Islam itself, there are intense debates about what constitutes a proper relationship between men and women. The Qur'an, considered to be the final and complete word of Allah (God), states that men and women are equal spiritually and should be equally respected and valued. However, because society is imperfect, there must be clear rules for proper living. One of these is modest dress for both sexes so that sexual attraction does not become the focus of life. The Qur'an says only that women should cover their chests and other necessary parts whenever a man other than an immediate family member is present. What is "necessary" is debated, ranging from light coverings to protect from the sun to head-to-toe veiling to protect from the leering gazes of men, but the Qur'an does not say that women should be veiled in any particular way.

Another Muslim practice outlined in the Qur'an is polygamy, the taking of as many as four wives. Polygamy was originally a way for wealthy men to give legal standing to widows with no male protector and to ensure many children. However, the Qur'an is clear that a man must be able to give good, and equal, financial and emotional care to all his wives. Because this is difficult, the Qur'an actually recommends monogamy. Even when married, women have many legal rights, including the ability to maintain separate property.

Many people claim that the Qur'an gives men permission to beat their wives, or even kill them if they are unfaithful. In fact, the Qur'an says a man must talk over marital problems with his wife. If she is unfaithful, he may strike her in a way that does not do physical injury. The meaning of "strike" has been hotly debated, but more liberal Muslims point out that the Qur'anic idea of marriage as a partnership of spiritual equals would preclude real physical violence.

Cultures vary widely, and as a result the Qur'an is interpreted very differently from place to place. Often these interpretations result in gross mistreatment of women if the tendency is already there in tribal custom. Many Muslims are horrified by what they perceive as the misuse of the Qur'an to justify brutality. They are also concerned about the bad image the behavior of some Muslims gives their religion as a whole.

EDUCATION

A desire for an Islam-centered nation, and disagreements about what this means, will also affect the educational system of the newly rebuilt country. Today, the educational system is in ruins. Literacy, especially among girls, is low because they were forbidden to attend school. Boys have suffered as well because most teachers are female, and the Taliban forbade them to work. The only education most boys have received is in *madrasas,* religious schools dedicated to teaching interpretations of the Qur'an that encourage hostility toward the United States and its allies and resistance to the influence of anything considered Western.

Poor education has had two effects that, even if effectively addressed by the new government, will have repercussions long into the future. The first effect is that a generation of Afghans is largely illiterate. Close to half of the population (42 percent) is fourteen years of age or younger. By some estimates, only a little over 10 percent of these children can read and write well, and they will soon be the generation on which the nation depends. Future teachers, doctors, engineers, government officials, and others must come from this generation. Whether the problem of the current young generation's illiteracy can ever be effectively addressed is questionable because they are already adults in terms of their responsibilities to their families and communities. They are getting ready to marry and raise families, clear and replant fields, rebuild the rubble of their homes, and reopen trade with other communities. They are not likely to find time for school.

Furthermore, democracies require that people form and express their own opinions. Illiteracy, however, breeds unquestioning attitudes that allow oppressive governments to take hold, and this will be a continued risk in Afghanistan. Change is frightening, and many Afghans may not like the way their lives are disrupted by it. In the future, there are likely to be new forces that promise a return to stability, just as the Taliban did, and they will find greater support among the uneducated than elsewhere. This will continue to pose a threat to the development of democracy in the country.

The second troubling effect of the poor state of schooling is the mind-set of those who have gone to *madrasas.* Their thinking has been deliberately shaped to perceive the Western world, particularly the United States, as corrupt and godless.

They have been taught to see themselves as warriors in a jihad against this corruption and that Allah smiles on any effort they make in this regard. As a result, many young Afghan boys today, as well as young men already done with school and out in the world, have a deeply ingrained sense of right and wrong and a sense of divine mission that is at odds with much of the rest of the world. Young Afghan men educated in the *madrasas* are not likely to change their minds about the appropriateness of inflicting great harm around the world and at home in the name of Allah; nor are they likely to have any desire to participate in a Western-style democracy. To them, the Taliban was doing a great service to their country and the world, and they are likely to work against the peaceful development of Afghanistan and the continued domination of the United States and other Western powers.

These two legacies, illiteracy and indoctrination, are beyond the power of any government to change because the damage has already been done. It is the next generation that will be shaped by what the Karzai and future governments do today. The role of the Qur'an in school will be an issue, because it is through that text that Islamic values are taught, but there is little agreement about what those values should be. What should

A Muslim teacher explains the Qur'an to young boys at a madrasas, *the only place education was taught under the Taliban regime.*

girls be trained to do? How should boys be taught to act? What do all children need to learn to be good Afghan citizens and productive members of society? It is hard to know the answers to these questions when there is no clear, shared vision about where the country should be headed.

HEALTH AND SOCIAL SERVICES

Far more concrete is what the country needs to do immediately to provide desperately needed social services to its people. The health of Afghans is very poor. The average life expectancy is a shocking forty-six years, approximately thirty fewer than in the United States. Lack of fresh water, poor sanitation, and inadequate diets have contributed to Afghanistan having the highest child mortality rate in the world, largely from diseases and conditions such as diarrhea, pneumonia, and measles that could be easily cured if treatment were available. However, the health care system in Afghanistan is in shambles due to decades of war and recent Taliban decrees that allowed some women to work as nurses, doctors, and aides but did not allow both sexes

Hoisting bags of food and seed provided by the United States, Afghan men carry relief to their people.

to be in a room together or allow male doctors to examine female patients except through their burkahs. Now that such restrictions have been lifted, hospital and clinic facilities and equipment will need to be brought to an operational level to begin to serve all those in need of medical attention.

Coordinated social services are also needed to bring food to those who have been driven from their homes or are unable to tend animals and plant and harvest crops because of wartime conditions. People will also need assistance with such things as seeds to plant crops, animals to restock herds, and tools to reopen wells and rebuild bombed-out irrigation systems. An estimated ten thousand villages and their surroundings were destroyed by decades of bombs and shelling, and homes, as well as schools, clinics, and other community buildings, will need to be rebuilt. These and other human services are the focal point of much international aid, particularly by the United States, which has come to understand how its fleeting interest in Afghanistan during the cold war created the climate in which the Taliban and terrorism could flourish. During that conflict, in the words of Ahmed Rashid in his acclaimed work *Taliban*, the United States was "prepared to fight till the last Afghan to get even with the Soviet Union, but when the Soviets left . . . [it] was not prepared to help bring peace or feed a hungry people."[21] The United States is determined not to make the same mistake twice.

BUILDING A SELF-SUSTAINING ECONOMY AND ENVIRONMENT

By global standards, Afghanistan is a poor nation at the best of times, and rebuilding it will be a massive undertaking. Among the problems facing future governments is strengthening the economic infrastructure so that businesses, from the stall vendor in the local bazaar to the large industries that Afghanistan must attract, will be able to make profits that can be funneled back into the country's economy. A stable government with a functioning legal system will be the foundation for encouraging the development of businesses. Likewise, Afghans must begin creating goods for export and find outlets for those exports. Mining ores and gems, as well as establishing manufacturing companies to make products such as cars, shoes, and other consumer goods for world markets, can be developed to improve the balance of trade. Today, Afghanistan imports far more than it exports, and this creates spiraling debt. This situation must improve or the country will remain not only very poor but dependent on foreign aid and thus unable to focus on its own best interests when they come in conflict with those of richer nations. However, manufacturing and mining must be undertaken carefully. Foreign corporations that come to developing countries often end up exploiting poor workers and badly damaging the environment with air, water, and soil pollution.

Severe environmental damage, however, has already been done by decades of war. Not only have large amounts of the country been blown up, burned, or otherwise destroyed, but desperate people have done things to survive that have made the situation worse. At present, only about half of the already less than 15 percent of usable agricultural land is being cultivated. In the past two decades alone, approximately 35 percent of arable land was lost, and agricultural production fell by half. Out of desperation, and often because of intimidation by local warlords, some farmers turned to growing opium poppies and others began clear-cutting forests to sell the timber illegally over the border in Pakistan. According to environmentalist Daud Saba, forest restoration "may take more than a century, if possible at all." [22] People also tore down wild pistachio groves because their roots were valuable for a medicinal remedy popular among Pakistanis. Likewise, mulberry and other fruit groves have been destroyed for firewood, further undermining Afghans' ability to feed themselves in the future. Another problem has been caused by the expansion of cities. Because they have usually sprung up near arable land, when suburbs take over fertile fields, much-needed agricultural land is lost. With so many displaced people returning from refugee camps, cities are likely to continue their sprawl, creating further loss of potential land for crops.

Yet another environmental issue is at the forefront of Afghans' attention. Decades of war have left Afghanistan littered with more than 10 million land mines, making it, according to Daud Saba, "the world's deadliest minefield." [23] An estimated twenty to thirty people die each day as a result of walking on mines of various sorts, including tiny Soviet butterfly mines that Saba says "floated down from the helicopters and then lay in wait for unmindful children and animals." [24] Particularly hard hit have been nomads who must move freely across large stretches of land and farmers who don't want to risk plowing their fields. Because the mines were dropped indiscriminately instead of being mapped

THE WORLD'S LARGEST PRODUCER OF OPIUM

During the last few decades, when many Afghans became unable to survive by growing their traditional crops, some turned to other means of making a living: growing opium poppies. According to Afghan environmentalist Daud Saba, in "Afghanistan's Natural Heritage: Problems and Perspectives," the cultivation of opium "was encouraged by market economy and assisted by Afghan warlords and the international growing drug market." Today, as a result, Afghanistan is the world's top producer of opium, the raw material for heroin, contributing a staggering 75 percent of the total amount on the world market.

This creates a number of problems that will hinder Afghanistan's economic recovery. First, when opium poppies yield more money to the farmers than dietary staples such as barley, wheat, and rice, it will be difficult to get many farmers to choose to grow the food the country so desperately needs. The cultivation of opium poppies also leads to violence among well-armed drug rings, adding to the misery of ordinary Afghans' lives. Furthermore, having an addictive drug available has proven irresistible to some people. According to Saba, before 1995 "we could rarely see a heroin addict in our society [but] today it is a major drug used by our youth." As a side effect, AIDS cases are now surfacing in Afghanistan for the first time, primarily from the use of dirty needles.

Interestingly, because heroin and opium were not specifically mentioned in the Qur'an, the Taliban chose to ignore the obvious fact that prohibitions on drinking alcohol should logically be extended to use of these drugs. Although the Taliban officially banned all aspects of the production of opium, rather than destroying the crops it simply taxed them to give it money to wage its wars against the people of Afghanistan.

Militant warlords harvest opium poppies.

for easier removal later, it is difficult to even estimate how long it will be before it is safe to simply walk across fields or clear the rubble of buildings. Even with a concerted effort to remove the mines, people will continue to be maimed or killed by them for many years to come.

AFGHANISTAN IN THE GLOBAL COMMUNITY

Afghanistan faces an immense set of internal challenges, but it is also a part of a larger community. First, whatever happens to Afghanistan will have a major effect on the future of Central Asia, the Middle East, and the Indian subcontinent. This area is politically unstable as a result of the change in the balance of power after the fall of the Soviet Union and the rise of Islamic fundamentalism. If a strong democracy evolves in Afghanistan, it could become a leader in establishing more widespread peace and stability in the region. If it falls back into civil war, it will once again be torn by the interests of richer and more powerful outsiders, just as it was when the Soviets invaded and when the well-financed al-Qaeda was able to set up its organization on Afghan territory.

It is now increasingly clear that what happens in Afghanistan's part of the world will also have a major impact on the well-being of everyone else on the planet. No one understands this better than Hamid Karzai and his cabinet. As he said in his inauguration speech, "The significance of this day in Afghan history will really depend on what happens in the future. If we deliver what we promise to the Afghan people, this will be a great day. If we don't deliver, we'll go to oblivion."[25] Karzai has in his favor, however, the fact that his fellow Afghans are strong and resilient people, not given to despair and willing to work extraordinarily hard. Added to that is the fact that the rest of the world sees more clearly than ever before the impact of any one nation on the destiny of the rest.

Afghanistan has, at times, been isolated from the main currents of international politics, economics, and history, but it is now back on center stage, just as when East and West met and traded in the bazaars of the Silk Road. A new, more collaborative perspective is needed today, and the words of Abdur Rahman Khan spoken to his people at the dawn of the twentieth century seem equally true at the dawn of the twenty-first: "The first and most important advice that I can give to my successors and people . . . is to impress upon their minds that unity and unity alone can make Afghanistan into a great power."[26] But unity also has taken on a global dimension. What happens now to Afghanistan will not only affect the future stability and prosperity of Central Asia and the Middle East but also help to shape, for better or worse, the future of the entire world.

Facts About Afghanistan

Numerical data about the population and economy are often not available, contradictory, inaccurate, or estimates. Most of these figures are provided by the *CIA World Factbook* based on the best available information as of the year 2000.

Geography

Total area: 250,775 square miles (slightly smaller than Texas)

Border countries: China, Iran, Pakistan, Tajikistan, Turkmenistan, Uzbekistan

Terrain: Mostly mountains, with plains and deserts in the western regions

Climate: Arid to semiarid, with cold winters and hot summers

Natural resources: Natural gas, petroleum, coal, copper and other ores, and gemstones

Land use:

    Arable land: 12% (4% under cultivation), 30,000 square kilometers

    Permanent pastures: 46%

    Forests and woodland: 3%

    Other: 39%

Natural hazards: Earthquakes, flooding, and drought

Environmental issues: Soil degradation, overgrazing, deforestation, desertification, and land mines

People

Population: 16–22 million (figures vary due to the fluid number of refugees)

    0–14 years: 42%

    15–64 years: 55%

    65 years and older: 3%

Birthrate: 41 births/1,000 population

Infant mortality: 147 deaths/1,000 live births

Life expectancy: 46 years

Total fertility rate: 6 children per woman

Ethnic groups: Pashtun, 38% (but other sources suggest it may be closer to 50%); Tajik, 25%; Hazara, 19%; Uzbek, 6%; other, 12%

Religions: Sunni Muslim, 84%; Shiite Muslim, 15%; other, 1%

Languages: Pashto, Dari, and Arabic (for religious services)

Literacy (those age 15 or over who can read and write):

> Total population: 31%
>> Male: 47%
>> Female: 15%

GOVERNMENT

Government type: Until December 2001, no internationally recognized, functioning central government; as of December 2001, an internationally recognized interim coalition government led by Hamid Karzai and a twenty-nine-member cabinet

Capital: Kabul

Administrative divisions: 30 provinces

Constitution: None

Legal System: No officially adopted system; shari'a (Islamic law determined by council of mullahs) in place under Taliban

Suffrage: None; previously limited to males between 15–50 years of age

Executive branch: Until December 2001, the country had no central government and was divided among fighting factions, with the Taliban controlling 80 percent of the country. The United Nations continued to recognize the previous government of Burhanuddin Rabbani, and Afghanistan's seat on various world and regional councils was left vacant since the Taliban takeover. As of December 2001, Hamid Karzai is prime minister for a six-month period until elections can be held in 2002.

Legislative branch: Nonfunctioning as of June 1993

Judicial branch: No upper courts functioning as of 1996; local shari'a or Islamic courts established throughout the country

Chief political parties and leaders in 2001:

> Taliban
>> Mullah Mohammad Omar

> United National Islamic Front for the Salvation of Afghanistan (UNIFSA, a coalition of thirteen parties opposed to the Taliban)
>> Burhanuddin Rabbani, chairman
>> General Abdul Yashid Dostam, vice chairman
>> Ahmad Shah Masood, military commander (killed September 2001)
>> Mohammad Yunis Qanuni, spokesperson

ECONOMY

Gross domestic product (GDP): $21 billion

GDP per capita income: $800

GDP by sector:

> Agriculture: 53%
> Industry: 28.5%
> Services: 18.5%

Labor force by occupation (1990 estimate):

Agriculture: 70%

Industry: 15%

Services: 15%

Industries: Small-scale production of textiles, soap, furniture, shoes, fertilizer, hand-woven carpets, natural gas, oil, coal, and copper

Agricultural products and exports: Opium poppies, wheat, fruits, nuts, wool, mutton, and animal pelts

Exports: $80 million (does not include opium trade)

Imports: $150 million in food, petroleum products, and consumer goods

Notes

Introduction: Afghanistan at the Crossroads

1. Jason Elliot, *An Unexpected Light: Travels in Afghanistan.* New York: Picador Press, 1999, p. 333.

Chapter 1: The Shape of a Nation: Land and People

2. "Afghanistan." Munich, Germany: Nelles Maps, 2001.

Chapter 3: In the Crossfire of World History

3. Pankaj Mishra, "The Making of Afghanistan," *New York Review of Books,* November 15, 2001. www.nybooks.com.

4. Quoted in Mishra, "The Making of Afghanistan."

5. Sarah Boxer, "An Archive of Images Details Afghanistan's Pre-Taliban Void," *New York Times on the Web,* October 2, 2001. www.nytimes.com.

Chapter 4: The Rise and Fall of the Taliban

6. Mishra, "The Making of Afghanistan."

7. Mishra, "The Making of Afghanistan."

8. Ralph H. Magnus and Eden Naby, *Afghanistan: Mullah, Marx, and Mujahid.* Boulder, CO: Westview Press, 2000, p. 182.

9. Magnus and Naby, *Afghanistan,* p. 182.

10. Quoted in Magnus and Naby, *Afghanistan,* p. 184.

11. Quoted in Tim Judah, "Profile: Mullah Mohammad Omar," *Guardian Unlimited Observer,* September 23, 2001. www.observer.co.uk.

12. Quoted in Mishra, "The Making of Afghanistan."

13. Quoted in Judah, "Profile: Mullah Mohammad Omar."

CHAPTER 5: LIFE IN TODAY'S AFGHANISTAN

14. Boxer, "An Archive of Images Details Afghanistan's Pre-Taliban Void."

15. Mishra, "The Making of Afghanistan."

16. Sirdar Ikbal Ali Shah, *Afghanistan of the Afghans.* London: Octagon Press, 1982, p. 37.

17. Quoted in Michael Fathers, "Frozen in Time," *Sabawoon,* October 4, 2001. www.sabawoon.com.

CHAPTER 6: THE CROSSROADS OF ART AND CULTURE

18. Quoted in "Introduction to Afghan Music," *Radio Afghanistan,* February 2001. www.radioafghanistan.com.

19. Nabi Kohzad, "Ancient Musical Instruments of Afghanistan," trans. Farhad Azad, *Lemar-Aftaab,* October–December 1997. www.afghanmagazine.com.

CHAPTER 7: FACING THE FUTURE: CONTEMPORARY CHALLENGES

20. Quoted in Kathy Gannon, "Karzai Sworn in as Afghan Premier," *CompuServe News,* December 22, 2001. www.compuserve.com/news/story.

21. Ahmed Rashid, *Taliban: Militant Islam, Oil, and Fundamentalism in Central Asia.* New Haven, CT: Yale Nota Bene Press, 2000, p. 209.

22. Daud Saba, "Afghanistan's Natural Heritage: Problems and Perspectives," *Lemar-Aftaab,* January–December 2001. www.afghanmagazine.com.

23. Saba, "Afghanistan's Natural Heritage."

24. Saba, "Afghanistan's Natural Heritage."

25. Quoted in Babak Dehghanpisheh and Ron Moreau, "The Toughest Job in the World," *MSNBC.com,* December 27, 2001. www.msnbc.com.

26. Quoted in "Quotes from Afghan Personalities of Yesterday and Today," *Afghan Web,* December 11, 2001. www.afghan-web.com.

GLOSSARY

anarchy: A breakdown of governmental control characterized by widespread lawlessness and disorder.

arable: Capable of being cultivated for crops.

fundamentalism: The belief that one should strictly and literally adhere to the words of a holy text.

indigenous: Native; originating or naturally occurring in a particular place.

Islamism: The belief that Islam, as described and dictated by the words of the Qur'an, can serve as the basis for the political, economic, legal, and military practices and decisions of a country.

jihad: Arabic word for "holy war," referring not only to armed resistance against people and practices considered unholy, but also to maintaining personal vigilance against unholy influences in one's own life.

Loya Jirgah: A tribal assembly of Pashtun groups.

madrasa: A school focusing on teaching the Qur'an and its applications in society.

Marxism: A political and economic system, closely related to communism, focusing on communal rather than individual effort, responsibility, and reward for labor.

militia: A small, armed group operating independently of a national army.

mujahideen: Islamic fighters against oppressive governments, from the Arabic for "those who struggle" or "those who strive."

mullah: A formally trained teacher of the Qur'an and Islam.

purdah: The practice of keeping women confined in their homes.

shari'a: A system of law derived entirely from the words of the Qur'an.

Shiite: One of the two major branches of Islam.

steppe: High-altitude plains covered with grasses and low shrubs.

Sunni: One of the two major branches of Islam.

CHRONOLOGY

ca. 2000 B.C.
Mundigak (near present-day Qandahar) and Kabul established.

1400–600 B.C.
Zarathustra brings Zoroastrianism to Bactria, the kingdom of Vishtaspa, part of present-day Afghanistan (dates disputed).

522–486 B.C.
The Achaemenian dynasty is at its peak during the rule of Darius the Great.

329 B.C.
The Achaemenian dynasty is overthrown by Alexander the Great, bringing Greek influence to the region.

323 B.C.
Alexander the Great dies; the united region soon splinters.

A.D. 50
The rule of Kaniska is the height of the Kushan dynasty, bringing Buddhist culture to the region.

652
Arabs introduce Islam in Afghanistan; after initial resistance, widespread conversion is accomplished by the late 800s.

962
The first Muslim dynasty, the Ghaznavids, is established by Alptegin.

998–1030
The rule of Mahmud extends the kingdom to the Punjab in modern-day Pakistan.

1140
The Ghaznavid dynasty falls to Ghurids.

1219
Genghis Khan and the Mongol army invade Afghanistan.

1370
Timur invades Afghanistan, establishing the Timurid dynasty, the golden age of Islamic culture.

1504–1519
Babur takes control of Kabul and establishes the Mogul empire; the center of the empire gradually shifts to northern India, leaving Afghanistan on the margins.

1520–1579
Bayazid Roshan leads a series of revolts against Mogul power.

1622
The Persian empire takes control of the area around Qandahar.

1708
Mir Wais reestablishes Afghan control of Qandahar.

1722
Mir Muhammad invades Persia.

1732–1739
Persian emperor Nader Shah occupies all of Afghanistan and eventually much of northern India.

1747
Nader Shah is assassinated; Ahmad Shah founds the Durrani dynasty.

1747–1773
Under the rule of Ahmad Shah, Durrani the Afghan empire is at its largest, extending from Kashmir to the Arabian Sea.

1773–1826
Anarchy and revolts occur under a succession of weak kings.

1826
Dost Mohammad Khan takes the throne from Mahmud Shah and establishes the Barakzai dynasty, Afghanistan's last.

1840
The first Anglo-Afghan War starts; Dost Mohammad is exiled.

1842
"Puppet" king Shojais killed; British garrison is destroyed in Khyber Pass.

1843

The first Afghan war ends; Dost Mohammad retakes the throne.

1863

Dost Mohammad dies; Sher Ali takes the throne.

1873

A treaty with Russia establishes Afghanistan's northern border.

1878

The second Anglo-Afghan War starts.

1879

The Battle of Maiwand triggers the end of the second Afghan War; Sher Ali dies.

1880

Abder Rahman Khan takes the throne.

1893

The Durand line fixes the eastern border of Afghanistan.

1919

Amanollah takes the throne.

1919–1921

The third Afghan war occurs; the Treaty of Rawalpindi ends British control of Afghan foreign affairs.

1929

Amanollah is deposed by Bacha-I-Saqao; Nader Khan takes the throne.

1933

Nader Khan is assassinated; Zahir Shah (the last king) takes the throne.

1947

Great Britain withdraws from India; Pakistan is created out of Indian-held and traditional Pashtun lands.

1961

A near–civil war occurs over the issue of Pashtunistan.

1964

A constitutional monarchy is declared.

1965

The Afghan Communist Party secretly forms.

1973
Zahir Shah is deposed; Afghanistan is declared a republic; the
Marxist era begins; Mohammad Daud becomes president.

1975
The mujahideen insurrections begin.

1978
Daud is murdered; Mohammad Taraki is declared president.

1979
Taraki is murdered; the Soviets invade Afghanistan; Hafizullah
Amin is murdered.

1989
The Soviets withdraw from Afghanistan.

1992
The Marxist regime falls to mujahideen in Afghanistan;
Burhanuddin Rabbani is installed as president.

1994
Mullah Omar founds the Taliban in response to anarchy
caused by the struggle for control of the government between Rabbani and Hekmatyar factions.

1996
The Taliban takes control of Kabul, establishing itself as the
governing body for most of Afghanistan.

1998
U.S. cruise missiles attack terrorist camps inside Afghanistan.

1999
The United Nations imposes sanctions on Afghanistan.

2001
Stone Buddhas at Bamian are blown up, along with other
relics and sites; the World Trade Center and Pentagon in
the United States are attacked, setting in motion air strikes
on Afghanistan; the Taliban falls; Hamid Karzai is sworn in
as interim prime minister.

FOR FURTHER READING

BOOKS

Sharifah Eniyat, *Cultures of the World: Afghanistan.* Tarrytown, NY: Marshall Cavendish, 1995. Good, but somewhat basic discussion.

Edward Grazda, *Afghanistan Diary.* New York: Powerhouse Books, 2000. Primarily black-and-white photographs, augmented with short essays, this book shows clearly what life in Afghanistan has been like in recent years.

Bob Italia, *Afghanistan.* Minneapolis, MN: Abdo and Daughters, 2002. New publication with useful information.

Rukhsana Khan, *Muslim Child.* Toronto, Ontario: Napoleon Publications, 1999. Acclaimed book written for North American Muslim and non-Muslim children describing the tenets of Islam and the experience of being a Muslim today.

———, *The Roses in My Carpets.* New York: Holiday House, 1998. Another work describing the life of Afghan children.

Lawrence McKay Jr., *Caravan.* New York: Lee and Low Books, 1995. Fictional account of a boy's first experience on a trading trip with his father through the mountains of Afghanistan.

Camille Mirepoix, *Afghanistan in Pictures.* Minneapolis, MN: Lerner Publications, 1997. Very basic text with some useful information.

Sheila Paine, *Afghan Amulet: Travels from the Hindu Kush to Razgrad.* New York: St. Martin's Press, 1994. Very readable and interesting book describing a woman's adventures in Afghanistan and neighboring countries while looking for the origin of a design on a dress.

Louis Palmer, *Adventures in Afghanistan.* London, UK: Octagon Press, 1990. Description of the author's experiences among the mujahideen and elsewhere in Afghanistan in the 1980s.

Amanda Roraback, *Afghanistan in a Nutshell.* Santa Monica, CA: Enisen, 2001. Useful twenty-four-page summary of information about Afghanistan.

WEBSITES

Afghan Land (www.afghanland.com). One of many websites devoted to information about Afghanistan.

Afghanpedia (www.afghanpedia.com). Another website devoted to information about Afghanistan.

ArianaAfghan (www.arianaafghan.com). Online magazine devoted to Afghan arts and culture.

ArianaE (www.arianae.com). A good site devoted to Afghan culture and news.

WORKS CONSULTED

BOOKS

Simon Broughton et al., *World Music: The Rough Guide*. London: Rough Guides Unlimited, 1994. Thorough work with a chapter on the popular and traditional music of Afghanistan.

Jason Elliot, *An Unexpected Light: Travels in Afghanistan*. New York: Picador Press, 1999. Excellent combination of travel narrative and analysis of the culture and history of Afghanistan.

Y. V. Gankovsky et al., *A History of Afghanistan*. Moscow: Progress Publishers, 1982. This book written by Soviet scholars provides a different and informative perspective on Afghanistan history up to and including the Soviet occupation.

Ralph H. Magnus and Eden Naby, *Afghanistan: Mullah, Marx, and Mujahid*. Boulder, CO: Westview Press, 2000. Definitive work by noted scholars on the historical, sociological, economic, and political forces affecting Afghanistan today.

Peter Manuel, *Popular Musics of the Non-Western World*. New York: Oxford University Press, 1988. Contains a short but informative discussion of Afghan music.

Ahmed Rashid, *Taliban: Militant Islam, Oil, and Fundamentalism in Central Asia*. New Haven, CT: Yale Nota Bene Press, 2000. Acclaimed book describing the inner workings and history of the Taliban.

Malcolm B. Russell, *The Middle East and Southeast Asia 2000*. Harpers Ferry, VA: Stryker-Post, 2000. Short profiles of all countries in the region, including a clear, focused, and thorough presentation of Afghanistan.

Sirdar Ikbal Ali Shah, *Afghanistan of the Afghans*. London: Octagon Press, 1982. Classic work describing what the cultural life of Afghanistan was like before the disruptions of recent decades.

Internet Sources

"Afghani Fighters," December 24, 2001. www.csun.edu.

Muhammed Asadi, "Rewriting the History of Women's Rights," December 29, 2001. www.geocities.com.

Farhad Azad, "Ahmad Zahir: The Golden Voice," *Lemar-Aftaab*, December 24, 2001. www.afghanmagazine.com.

"Backgrounder on Afghanistan: History of the War," *Backgrounder*, October 23, 2001. www.hrw.org/backgrounder.

Sarah Boxer, "An Archive of Images Details Afghanistan's Pre-Taliban Void," *New York Times on the Web*, October 2, 2001, www.nytimes.com.

Babak Dehghanpisheh and Ron Moreau, "The Toughest Job in the World," *MSNBC.com*, December 27, 2001. www.msnbc.com.

Michael Fathers, "Frozen in Time," *Sabawoon*, October 4, 2001. www.sabawoon.com.

Kathy Gannon, "Karzai Sworn in as Afghan Premier," *CompuServe News*, December 22, 2001. www.compuserve.com/news/story.

"Introduction to Afghan Music," *Radio Afghanistan*, February 2001. www.radioafghanistan.com.

Tim Judah, "Profile: Mullah Mohammad Omar," *Guardian Unlimited Observer*, September 23, 2001. www.observer.co.uk.

Nabi Kohzad, "Ancient Musical Instruments of Afghanistan." Trans. Farhad Azad, *Lemar-Aftaab*, October–December 1997. www.afghanmagazine.com.

Richard Lacayo, "Behind the Veil," *Time*, December 3, 2001. www.time.com.

Preston Mendenhall, "Afghans Ponder Life After the Taliban," *MSNBC.com*, October 24, 2001. www.msnbc.com.

———, "Soap Opera Escape for Afghans," *MSNBC.com*, October 29, 2001. www.msnbc.com.

Pankaj Mishra, "The Making of Afghanistan," *New York Review of Books*, November 15, 2001. www.nybooks.com.

Michael Moran, "Bin Laden Comes Home to Roost," *MSNBC.com*, August 24, 1998. www.msnbc.com.

"Mullah Nasruddin," December 29, 2001. www.afghan-net work.net.

Fabriba Nawa, "Khoshnawaz Brothers Keep Herat's Music Alive," *Lemur-Aftaab,* January–December 2001, www.afghan magazine.com.

"Quotes from Afghan Personalities of Yesterday and Today," *Afghan Web,* December 11, 2001. www.afghan-web.com.

A. F. J. Remy, "The Avesta," *Catholic Encyclopedia,* December 12, 2001. www.newadvent.org.

"Reuter's AlertNet: Afghanistan," December 2001. www.alert net.org.

Daud Saba, "Afghanistan's Natural Heritage: Problems and Per- spectives," *Lemar-Aftaab,* January–December 2001. www.afghanmagazine.com.

WEBSITES

Afghan Info (www.afghan-info.com). Excellent, thorough web- site with a wide range of articles and links.

Afghanistan Online (www.afghan-web.com). One of the most thorough and reliable websites offering a wide range of arti- cles on politics, history, culture, and other issues, plus many links to other sites.

Afghan Radio (www.afghanradio.com). Good site for current events.

CIA World Factbook: Afghanistan (www.odci.gov/cia/ publications/factbook). Online condensed version of statis- tical and other information available in book form from the Central Intelligence Agency.

Islamic Studies, Islam, Arabic, and Religion (www.uga.edu/islam). Website of Professor Alan Godlas, of the University of Georgia Department of Arabic and Religion; a thoughtful and thor- oughly researched source of information.

Lemar-Aftaab (www.afghanmagazine.com). Excellent site fo- cusing primarily on the arts and current issues.

Lonely Planet World Guide: Afghanistan (www.lonelyplanet. com). Good basic information on geography, history, and culture.

Sabawoon (www.sabawoon.com). Good site for some information, but somewhat erratically maintained and spotty.

Submission (www.submission.org). A very well researched and maintained site about all issues relating to Islam.

INDEX

PICTURE CREDITS

ABOUT THE AUTHOR

Laurel Corona lives in Lake Arrowhead, California, and teaches English and humanities at San Diego City College. She has a master's degree from the University of Chicago and a Ph.D. from the University of California at Davis. Dr. Corona has written many other books for Lucent Books, including *Brazil, Ethiopia, Life in Moscow, Peru,* and *The World Trade Center.*